OPPORTUNITIES IN
THEATRICAL DESIGN AND PRODUCTION

Ann Folke
Richard Harden

VGM Career Horizons
A Division of National Textbook Company
4255 West Touhy Avenue
Lincolnwood, Illinois 60646-1975 U.S.A.

ACKNOWLEDGMENTS

The authors gratefully acknowledge the generous assistance of the following in the preparation of this book: Arnold Abramson of Nolan Scenic Studios; Charlie Bellin; Peggy Clark; Harry Darrow; Lana Fritz; Darin Humecki; Donna Liebeman of Hudson Scenic Studios; Patrick Mann; Arthur Matera; Mitch Miller of Four Star Stage Lighting; John Nathan; Package Publicity Service; David Carl Robinson; Hillary Sherred; Paul Stenbach; Jack Stewart; Jean Webster; Marc B. Weiss; Terry H. Wells, Sharon White.

Photo Credits
Front cover: upper left, Wright State University, Dayton, OH, photo by Paul Harper; upper right and lower right, The Guthrie Theater; lower left, sound operator Chris Voellinger, The 46th Street Theater, Broadway.
Back cover: upper left, set designer J. Patrick Mann; upper right, production electrician Mitch Miller, Broadway's *Nine,* photo by Jack Stewart; lower left, Columbia College Chicago; lower right, stitcher Revka Tkach, New York, photo by Richard Harden.

ABOUT THE AUTHORS

Ann Folke has had an extensive career in acting, stage managing, and design which had its formal beginnings at Northwestern University where she received a bachelor's degree in theatre. She studied in the graduate school of theatre at Case-Western Reserve, and has been a long-time member of Actor's Equity, the American Theatre Association, and the U.S. Institute for Theatre Technology. She was a founding secretary of the Theatre Association of Pennsylvania.

Ms. Folke has played Gertrude in *The Summer House,* Miss Madrigal in *The Chalk Garden,* and Mrs. Alving in *Ghosts* for the Meat and Potatoes Theatre, New York; Rebecca West in *Rosmersholm,* at the University of Massachusetts, Amherst; The Maid in *Private Lives,* Poppy in *Tender Trap,* and Margaret in *Kind Sir* at the Country Club Theatre, Mt. Prospect, IL; the Maid in *Critics' Choice* at O'Hare Inn Theatre, Chicago; Madame Liang, *Flower Drum Song,* Sarah in *Paint your Wagon,* Melba in *Pal Joey,* and Bloody Mary in *South Pacific* for the Sullivan Playhouse, Sullivan, IL.

Among her stage managing and production credits are: light and set design, and stage managing for Sullivan Playhouse; set and light design and stage managing for Country Club Theatre; stage managing, Gene Frankel Theatre, the Meat and Potatoes Theatre, The Quaigh, and St. Clement's Theatre, all in New York, assitant to Jules Fisher in two shows on and two shows off Broadway. She was the stage manager for the premier of *Braindeath,* Cubiculo Theatre, New York.

She is also the Associate Editor of *Simon's Theatrical Directory,* and an Associate Editor of *Theatre, Design and Technology* magazine.

Richard Harden has developed his career through a broad range of experience in all kinds of theatre, including off-Broadway, regional, stock and university houses. He has served as director, production manager, casting director, stage manager, lighting designer, master electrician, and university technical director. His New York credits include *Lou,* at West End Theatre; *The Beethoven,* New World Theatre; *Rich and Famous,* Actors' Collective; *Little Bird,* for the New Dramatists; *Home Free!* at Circle Repertory; *Hole in the Wall* and *Click,* both at E.L.T. Lincoln Center; and *Aaron Burr* for the American Theatre Company.

His work in regional theatres includes *Crime on Goat Island,* for the Delaware Theatre Company; *Rainmaker* and *Lunch Hour* for the Mississippi Repertory Theatre; *Enter Laughing* at Salt City Center; *How the Other Half Lives,* Theatre by the Sea; *Moby Dick* at P.A.F. Playhouse, *To Kill a Mockingbird* and *World of Carl Sandburg* with the Indiana Repertory Theatre; and *The Dumbwaiter* at Purdue University.

He has also directed and stage managed many other shows; has served as Guest Instructor at New York University, as consultant to the Off-Off Broadway Alliance, and as Director with the New York State Arts Council Pilot Project.

He has a master's degree in directing from the University of Missouri-Kansas City, and has studied with the Acting Workshop with Michael Shurtleff, and the Directing Workshop with Marshall Mason.

FOREWORD

Designers and technicians give visual reality to the playwright's imagined setting in the theatre. They clothe actors in costumes and light, and can transport the audience to dazzling new realms, even in the instant that the curtain goes up.

Their magic is built upon the solid base of traditions developed over centuries, and is supported today by a contemporary magic of a different sort—one reflected in the latest developments in computers and electronic circuitry. As our society's technology expands, so also do the creative horizons of theatrical design. In addition, in a world in which many specializations have become increasingly narrow, the unusual potential for both artistic and technical creativity in theatrical design and production makes the careers in this field uniquely exciting and challenging.

Each of the many occupations in this field makes a distinct and necessary contribution to each new show; and with every new show each is provided the fresh potential for artistic and technical achievement. People who are exploring the possibility of futures in theatrical design and production will find this book to be a valuable guide to the many satisfying career choices available in this segment of the industry.

Margaret Lynn
Executive Director
American Theatre Association

PREFACE

The world today is in the midst of the greatest changes that it has seen in nearly two hundred years. All around us we find newer, faster, more automated approaches to every facet of our lives. The pioneers of the Industrial Revolution would be amazed at where their first steps are taking civilization. Computers now plan and execute vast portions of our jobs and our very lives. The lack of personal communication—the feeling of one-to-one contact—seems to be a minor lament of human beings all over the globe.

One area of life, one source of employment seems to be especially resistant to this trend. Theatre! Since long before the Industrial Revolution and surely for a long time yet to come, The Theatre reigns as a fundamental source of human independence and inter-involvement. The theatre, even as it seizes the latest developments of science and technology, remains one of the few areas in which the work of individual artisans continues to predominate.

Nearly all people have at one time or another wished that they could be someone else. They have wanted to be outrageously flamboyant, while they were actually rather shy. They have wanted to be terribly witty and urbane, when they were really prosaic and commonplace. It is this desire which provides the first contact with theatre for most people. Although it may lead them to acting, many people find out quickly that exposure in front of an audience is not their ideal, but this contact gives them the opportunity to discover the world backstage—production and design.

This book will attempt to isolate and illuminate the many possible careers involved in the production of any theatrical presentation. We will look at the creative world of the Designer. We will look at the work of planning, the building and the executing of all of the multi-faceted elements of the technician's world. And we will explore the managerial functions of the chief executive backstage—the Stage Manager.

—A.F. and R.H.

CONTENTS

Opening night on Broadway is characterized out front by lines of limousines, patrons, and onlookers; backstage, it is the scene of tightly controlled activity and concentration on the part of every professional. Photo: R. Harden.

CHAPTER 1

OPENING NIGHT ON BROADWAY

There is a nip of autumn in the air, as there should be at the beginning of a new theatre season, and a feeling of excitement, as there should be on opening night. The curtain, usually at 8:00 p.m., will rise at seven tonight, to give the drama critics an opportunity to prepare their reviews for the early morning editions.

Although some early-arriving members of the audience, dressed for a night out, are clustered in the lobby, the house isn't open yet for them to be seated. But why don't you follow along with us, and see what is going on?

The house-manager recognizes us, and lets us enter the empty auditorium, supplying you with a program from a stack inside the door. Opening it, you can see that this production is a musical, but one with only two actors. But we're not here to look at the actors tonight: we're here to get a look at the other jobs there are to do in the theatre. If you'll turn the pages of your program to the list of the *staff* (it's right there after the biographies of the author and the designers) you will see several dozen names of people without whom this opening could not be happening. And as we tour the house and the stage and watch the show, you'll meet more technicians who are helping make it happen.

Although the audience isn't here yet, the empty auditorium isn't really empty. There are two men at the very back of the top balcony, and there are circles of light playing about the stage and orchestra pit. These are the *Follow Spot Operators*. They will spend the show at the back of the balcony, operating those very large, powerful

1

spotlights, changing their colors, and in most of the musical numbers, following the stars on stage. Now they are testing their lights, and making sure that everything is ready. They may glance over the *cue sheets* that they have written during technical rehearsals, to make sure who their lights will follow, when, with how large a spot, and in what color.

It's not really hushed here, either. A voice is saying "Testing: one, two, three." We hear it through now one and then several of the speakers placed throughout the house. A man walks out from one of the proscenium doors, doors on either side of the stage that connect the audience and back stage areas. He walks to the back of the theatre where a black control panel with a great many knobs is curtained off. Since this is an older theatre built before sound control was housed in the audience, about eight theatre seats have been removed to accommodate the control panel. Our stars will be wearing cordless microphones. From this control panel, the *Sound Operator* will control the volume and quality of their voices. The sound operator may select the speakers from which the sound comes, and enhance it with echo or reverberation effects. Very likely some or all of the instruments in the orchestra will also be monitored, and their quality reinforced from this listening/control post.

Although the heavy velvet house curtain, or act curtain, will rise at the beginning of the overture to display the painted "show curtain" displaying the name of this musical, at the moment, both curtains are up. A man is on stage with a clipboard. As he calls out a number, a light comes on. This is the *Master Electrician*. Back stage left (that's the side of the stage to the actor's left as he or she faces the audience) another *Electrician* is pushing buttons on the console of a computerized lighting control system. They are double checking each of the several hundred stage lighting units that are to be used in our show, making sure that they go on, that they are the right color, and are still aimed ("focussed") at the correct part of the stage. Behind the Master Electrician, we hear calls of "heads" as curtains move up and down. The *Flyman* is making sure that the equipment for which he is responsible, curtains and pieces of scenery that go up and down or in and out on the stage, are working.

Let's go through the proscenium door, and see what else is going on backstage. Come into our office. It is a dressing room, up one flight of stairs on the stage left side, and it says "*STAGE MANAG-ERS*" on the door. There's a place to hang your coat, a file cabinet, a few piles of paper in wire baskets, and a pencil sharpener. Otherwise, with its mirrors surrounded by lights, it looks like just what it is, a dressing room. This is where the two of us, Ann the *Production Stage Manager* and Richard, the *Stage Manager,* along with David, the *Assistant Stage Manager,* do our book work and record-keeping. David seems to have gotten here before we did, and put the coffee on. Have a cup.

The first official task that we do after getting a very thick three-ring notebook out of one of the file drawers, is go down to the Call Board and sign in. The Call Board is a bulletin board near the Stage Door, the back stage entry to the theatre.

Although the actors are not required to be in the theatre until "half hour." (thirty minutes before curtain time), both of the members of our cast are here, as are their stand-bys, the performers who are ready to go on should one of the announced cast members be sick or unavailable. Should one of the cast members not be here, or not have called in, telling us that their doctor has told them that they cannot perform tonight (about the only excuse for missing a performance), it would be our job to alert the stand-by, who has already rehearsed the role with the director, and rehearsed it more with us. Should the stand-by go on, one of us is responsible for making the announcement of the replacement to the audience, and informing the house manager so that information about the replacement can be posted at the front of the theatre. But tonight is an opening, and all is well. Everyone in the cast is here.

Let's go meet the crew. The follow-spot operators and the sound operator are still out in the house. Back-stage here are the two electricians who were testing the lights when we came in. They have finished their light check, and are looking over their cue sheets by the lighting control system. Nearby is another Sound Operator, seated by a rack of reel to reel tape decks. There is "program sound" in this show— sound effects such as thunderstorms and traffic noises. This sound operator controls these sounds, which are on tape. They are fed to the master control console in the house, where, along with the reinforced sound, they are assigned to speakers. Were there fewer cues in the show, all of the sound might be controlled by the one operator in the house; but this is a "heavy" sound show. We have two operators in two places.

You will notice that there are four tape decks—at several times two sounds will be playing at once, one on each deck. The other two decks are stand-bys, each with a copy of the tape on it, each turning with a cue, so that, should a tape break, the operator has merely to switch to the stand-by. We try very hard to be prepared for any emergency.

The *fly gallery* is a metal grid corridor up one flight of stairs from the stage floor, and open to the stage. Up there, the flyman and his assistants have finished testing their lines. All of the pieces of flying scenery in the show are in working order.

Back down on the stage floor, the *Carpenter* finishes testing his equipment. The winches that move the heavy set pieces out on stage are in working condition. Other, smaller set pieces are stored, each exactly where it should be at the beginning or "top" of the show. The rest of the carpenter's crew, the *Grips,* are here, ready to work.

In the basement, next to the large room in which the orchestra is tuning up, the *Properties Mistress* and her assistant are preparing necessary refreshments. One of them is filling a liquor bottle with judicious amounts of apple juice and water (the actors in this production prefer that to cold tea), while the other is inspecting a tray of hor d'ouvres that has been ordered from a local restaurant, to be delivered before each performance. There is a small refrigerator in their room, and shelves containing replacements for the paper props that are used up each night, "understudy" props for fragile items that might get broken in use, and glues, paints and tools that might be needed for repairs. The properties people have checked all of the books, pillows, plants, dishes and bric-a-brac for which they are responsible. All of these "props" are in their proper place on the set, or on the off-stage prop tables. The crew has waited until now to deal with the food props, to keep them fresh.

On our way to the star dressing rooms to say hello to the cast, we pass the wardrobe room, where the *Wardrobe Mistress* is re-sewing the Scene Three costume, the one that often gets stepped on.

Now, we go to the Stage Manager's Desk, to test our equipment. Ann dons a headset, switches on the intercom, and pushes some buttons. Can she hear everyone, and can everyone hear her? The actors' voices assure us that she can be heard in the dressing rooms. We noticed when we visited the dressing rooms just now that the *monitor* system, which sends sounds from the stage to the dressing room, was working. We could hear the low conversation of the props people finishing their check. The sound operator says Ann can be heard, as do the electricians, the flyman, and David, the Assistant Stage Manager from the three posts off-stage left, right, and up center from which he will relay cues to the grips; they will move scenery. The *floor electricians* will connect electrical cables on moving pieces of scenery and activate the smoke effect and must also be able to hear their cues. The intercom system works. We don't have to ask the sound operator to do a quick repair. There is, of course, a stand-by system which we can activate during the show, should something go wrong with the primary system.

Just as the Properties Mistress is walking by the Stage Manager's Desk, the light connected to our telephone blinks. Answering it, we call to her. It is the restaurant manager, asking if the hor d'ouvres have arrived. She assures him that they have, reminds him that after tonight half hour will be at 7:30 Tuesday through Sunday, and 2:00 for the Wednesday and Saturday matinees. She also tells him to leave off the black olives—the leading lady hates them.

HALF HOUR

Ann pushes the button marked "All Stations" on the intercom control. "Good Evening, ladies and gentlemen," she says. "It is now half hour. Thirty minutes until curtain." A chorus of "thank yous" resounds in her ear. The only people running the show with whom she is not in direct communication are the follow spot operators. For some few musicals, and always for dance shows, they are also on headset. Most often they just watch the show and follow their cue sheets. Also answering her are the *House Electrician* and the *House Flyman*. These are the only people backstage who are employees of the theatre owners, rather than the producers of the show. The House Electrician controls the lights in the audience area, the "house lights"; the House Flyman will raise and lower the theatre's act curtain, or "house curtain". The House Electrician assures Ann that the house lights are on.

"We can open, as far as you're concerned, can't we?" she asks the Sound Operator in the house. The reply is yes. "Light check over?" she asks the Electric Department.

"Everything is clear in the front of the house," is the reply.

"O.K., Charlie," she says to the House Flyman, who is standing by the curtain ropes, next to the Stage Manager's desk. "Close the curtain." The great velvet drape is lowered. "Curtain Warmers," she says to Electrics. A lever is moved on the lighting control console. Warm rose light washes over the house curtain. Ann swivels slightly on her high stool, picks up a phone, and depresses a button.

The House Manager, seeing a light go on by his phone at the back of the theatre, picks up the receiver. "Can I open?" he asks, eagerly. "There's a lot of people out here."

"It's all yours," replies Ann. She turns back to the intercom. "Pre-set," she calls. "Clear the stage. Scenery coming in."

"Hold it a minute." This is from the Master Electrician, who is standing by the light tower on stage left.

"Flies, hold your pre-set," Ann calls. "What's the matter, Electrics?"

"A lamp burned out on the number one boom," the Electrician replies. "I've got it replaced, but I want to make sure I didn't knock the instrument out of focus. "Bring up dimmer 32," he calls to the other Electrician. The light goes on. The Master Electrician walks out onto the stage, stands with his arms held out in the beam of light, looking at his shadow. He goes back to the lighting instrument, loosens its clamp with his crescent wrench, makes a minimal adjustment, tightens it, walks back once again, calls to the control board to turn it off, and tells Ann that he is ready.

"O.K., now," says Ann. "Clear stage. Bring in the show curtain. Go."

The Flyman unlocks a set of lines downstage (stages used to slant from the back to the front, for purposes of sight lines; hence upstage is at the back of the stage, the top of the once incline, and downstage is close to the audience), and a brightly painted full stage drop fills the proscenium arch, just upstage of the act curtain. "Upstage limbo drop in," Ann calls. The upstage curtain that provides the backdrop for the first scene is lowered into position.

"Pre-set winches," she calls. The two parts of an elaborate, skeletal house lumber out onto the stage, their electric winch controls operated by two of the Electricians. Richard and David, standing by the Carpenters and on headset, have relayed Ann's cue to them.

The Properties People, one on each side of the set, are again checking that everything for which they are responsible is in the proper place. They have finished arranging on the off-stage tables all of the *hand props,* the packages, the suitcase, the fan and notebook that the actors carry on stage with them. Richard, with a copy of the prop list, is checking these. Everything is where it should be. Richard looks out onto the stage, and walks over to where the property assistant is placing a tall plastic rubber plant.

"I think," he says, "that it should be a little farther stage left. It has to be in front of the window when Charles walks past outside. Better change the spike." The Props Assistant pulls up a piece of tape on the floor, and puts it down securely a little to the left.

"Like that?"

"Perfect." Ann joins him on stage.

"I'm glad you caught that," she says. "And would you add to your check list, and tell props to make sure that the music box is set close to the leg of the hassock, with the hinges upstage. She picks it up in the dark, and it really bothers her if she has to turn it around while the lights are coming up."

Richard makes a note on his check list. As Ann walks back to her desk, she looks at her watch, which is always accurate. She, Richard and David usually start their working day by making a phone call to the correct time number.

"Fifteen minutes," she calls into the intercom. "Fifteen minutes, ladies and gentlemen. Fifteen minutes to curtain." Again, a chorus of "thank yous" is heard.

David, meanwhile, has circled the backstage area, a clipboard in hand, checking the pre-set of the smaller scenic units that will be

Character makeup may be designed by the actor or a makeup designer.
Here an actor adds shadows for an older man's face. Photo: Wright State
University, by Paul Harper.

used later in the show. He calls the Carpenter's attention to a screw slightly protuding from a hinge. "Can you get that in a little more?" he asks the Carpenter. "I'm afraid she'll catch her sleeve on it." The carpenter pulls a screw driver out of his pocket and complies. David also checks that the leading lady's second costume is laid out behind an off-stage screen, awaiting a quick change.

It is now ten minutes to curtain. The Properties Assistant has come to Ann, asking for a band-aid. He has a paper cut. Ann supplies the band-aid, and makes a note of the injury, albeit minor, on the Stage Manager's Nightly Report Sheet. The light on the phone to the front of the house flashes on, and Ann answers it.

"I don't suppose you're surprised," says the house manager's voice from the other end, "but we're going to have to hold. With the construction on the street, the cabs look like they're lined up to 5th Avenue. No more than five minutes, though."

Ann relays the delay to her cast and crew. "Ten minutes and holding," she calls.

"Thank you."

She opens a three ring notebook, which is labelled "Prompt Script," sets it on the sloped top of the Stage Manager's Desk, adjusts the lavender-gelled goose neck reading lamp so light doesn't spill onto the stage. Each right hand page of the prompt script is a page of dialogue or score of the musical. On each left hand page are diagrams of the actors' "blocking", the moves that they make on stage. Also marked on the left hand page are the technical cues; when there are lighting changes and sound effects, when curtains and scenery units move. As the orchestra leader conducts the actions of the players from a conductor's score, the Stage Manager will conduct and co-ordinate the performances of the actors and the technical crews. She glances at her pre-show check list, to see if she, Richard or David have double-checked that all of the elements of the production are in working order; and walks to the center of the stage, to check, once again, that everything is in readiness. As she leaves, the light goes on on the phone to the House Manager. Richard answers it. "All ready in five," says the House Manager.

Ann is back, and again on the intercom. "Five minutes," she calls. "Five minutes. Orchestra to the pit. Crew on stage. Five minutes, ladies and gentlemen. Five."

Voices on the head-set tell her that the crew is in position. The Assistant Conductor signals that the orchestra is ready. A final check is made with the house manager. She dispatches David to tell the Conductor to enter the pit. "Warn house to half," she calls to the House Electrician. "Overture. Places, ladies and gentlemen. Company on stage. Places please. Ready on house to half, warn house curtain, warn electrics one." She holds her hand on her stop watch. A surge of applause tells her that the conductor has made her entrance; a glimmer of blue-white light under the house curtain indicates that the follow spots are highlighting the conductor at her stand. Moments later, a signal light from the conductor tells the Stage Managers that the orchestra is ready. "House to half, GO," Ann calls. As the house lights are fading, Ann flicks a switch at her desk. A light goes on and off on the conductor's stand, indicating that all is ready backstage, and we are starting.

"Ready on house curtain. Ready on electrics one." The first sustained note of the overture is heard. Ann pushes the start button on her stop watch as she says "House curtain and electrics one, GO." The velvet act curtain lifts, revealing the painted show curtain; the lights hung from pipe towers in the house boxes (the "box booms") bathe it in color. By the midpoint of the overture, Ann has noted that, behind the curtain, both actors are ready, seated on the hassock downstage left. As the orchestra starts to play the quiet waltz theme, she calls for the house lights to be taken out. "And warn," she says, "warn electrics two, three, four, and five. Two, three and four are five counts. Cue five is a bump on the downbeat. Warn sound cue one. Warn fly cue one." The leading lady waves anxiously to David, who is standing stage left in the wings, beckoning him to her. In changing her position, she has caught a heel in her skirt and torn out a bit of the hem. She knows that it looks untidy, and she's afraid that it may trip her in the dance scene. David smiles at her. "Come on," he teases, "you'll have to find a harder problem than that." There is a short string of safety pins hanging from his shirt, awaiting just such an emergency. He repairs the damage, and as the orchestra begins the last thirty-two bars, returns to his off-stage post, making a mental note to be sure and tell the wardrobe mistress to make a more permanent repair in the skirt. Since he's been calm at his work, the mishap has not upset the actress.

CURTAIN GOING UP

As the music changed, Ann called "Ready on electrics two, three, four and five. Ready sound cue one. Ready fly cue one." The overture comes to an end. Ann notes the elapsed time, and listens to the applause crest. As the sound just starts to wane, she calls "Fly cue one, GO," and the show curtain flies out. It is a shade more than half-way out of sight when she calls, "Electrics two, GO."

Backlight, from instruments high and behind the set, aimed at the downstage, reveals the structure of the stage set in silhouette. The audience applause, which has barely died down from the overture, swells, acknowledging the opening picture on the stage, the work of the scenic and lighting designers. As this applause starts to die away, Ann calls, "Sound cue one, GO."

We hear a simple children's song being played on a music box.

Electrics cue three, GO," and a small pool of pale amber light seems to grow down stage left, illuminating our stars who are sitting on the hassock, listening to the prop music box. It doesn't really play, of course; the small, delicate sound of the melody is on tape, and plays through different speakers than those carrying the orchestra's overture.

Again the audience applause swells, acknowledging the appearance of our stars. Again Ann waits until the audience sound begins to decrease, and calls, "Electrics cue four, GO." More light fills the stage, revealing the room that the actors are in.

As they begin the dialogue that starts the show, David, on stage left, is following along in his script. It is very unlikely that the actors will forget a line and need to be prompted, but he is following the script closely, circling any words that are paraphrased, listening and watching that the actors are performing the musical as it was directed. All three stage managers, when we are not calling a cue or coping with an emergency, are watching the show. Although all three of us are backstage tonight, from now on either Ann or Richard will see the show from the house. Once a show has opened, it is our responsibility to preserve the work of the director. We can hold brush-up rehearsals with the cast once a week, if needed.

As we watch the show each night, we make notes of scenes or songs that might need work. Some of our "pick-ups" are simple notes that can be given to the actors at half hour: she should move a little stage left at the very beginning of the show so that she is fully in light, or they should both remember not to react to the music box until the sound can be heard.

The dialogue seems to be picking up a new, stacatto rhythm that subtly signals the beginning of a musical number. The reeds in the orchestra begin to play the music box melody in a simple underscoring. As the performers burst into song, Ann calls, "Electrics cue five, GO." The stage becomes brighter, the followspots pick up the two stars, and the show is underway.

Before each cue or action to be performed by the crews; sound, lights, carpenters, props or flies, the member of the Stage Management staff "calling the show" (relaying the cues over the headset) has called a "Warn," a "Ready," and a "Go." Sometimes, during a complicated ballet sequence, or during the transition from one scene to the next, there may be as many as twenty or thirty cues happening in rapid succession. "Warn Electrics twenty through thirty-two, Sound eight through twelve; warn Fly cues five, six and seven," would not be an unusual call.

During the operation of the cues, the Stage Managers are watching what is going on. Should anything go wrong, should anyone be in danger from a piece of flying scenery, should a set piece break or a light fail to come on, we must instruct the crews so that the problem is solved.

The fourth scene of our show is played downstage, in front of a stylized painted drop. While this scene is going on, behind the drop, the scenery is being set up for the dance hall sequence. There is now a wall in front of the skeletal structure that we saw at the opening of the show. The two sections on either end of the wall are hinged, and can pivot in towards the center of the stage, revealing the walls of the dance hall painted on their reverse sides. A bead curtain flies in to fill the space between them; a velvet curtain is flown in upstage of that. The velvet curtain is "masking," which prevents the audience from seeing the center part of the upstage wall. Tables, chairs, and a small platform with a piano on it are set in place. Ann has called the Fly cues at the proper time; the set-up looks complete.

Richard taps her shoulder to get her attention. "Vase," he says. There is a glass vase, with one rose on it, on one of the tables.

"Thank you. It had better go." At the end of the scene, the leading lady dances on that very small table. She would be likely to knock over the vase, perhaps breaking it, and hurting herself. "Props," she calls over the headset, "Strike the vase, please."

Neither she nor Richard can remove the vase. Properties may be handled only by the actors or the Properties crew. There is no answer over the headset. Richard moves upstage, and intercepts the Properties Mistress, who is exiting, having completed her set-up. "Could you please move the vase," he asks.

"Really?" she replies, "I thought it was back in."

"It's not." She darts back on stage and collects the prop. The set-up is complete.

Applause greets the end of the fourth scene. During the next twenty seconds, as the orchestra repeats the music box melody and slides are projected on the painted drop, both of our stars are changing their costumes. Their dressers are waiting for them in the wings; the costumes have been designed and constructed for fast changes. The movements of both the actors and the dressers are like a very precise dance.

Hat and cane down. Jacket off. Vest on. Old tie off. New tie on over the head and pulled tight. The drop flies out, and as the lights are coming up on the dance hall, our leading man has picked up his briefcase and a pencil from the Properties Mistress, and is standing by the piano. In the same amount of time, the leading lady has changed to a completely different dress. The dressers tidy up the areas where the changes happen, remove the last scene's costumes to the dressing room, and set up for their next change.

In a quiet moment, Ann makes a note about the vase. Perhaps the Scenic Designer, who had requested that Props put it there, had forgotten about the leading lady's dance on the table. Perhaps the Choreographer has changed the dance. It is a little problem, to be discussed with them tomorrow. In the mean time, at least there will not be broken glass on stage.

The pattern of calling "warns," and "readys," and "GOs," proceeds through the act. Scenery moves in and out; the stage is now darker, now lighter; dogs bark, smoke rises, costumes are changed. Each operation is instigated by the Stage Manager's call, and carried out by a member of a crew.

The music builds to a crescendo. There is a moment's silence; the gentle music box theme plays again, as Ann calls for the House Curtain and the House Lights. Act One is over. She stops her stopwatch, notes the elapsed time, and re-starts it, to keep track of the time of the intermission.

INTERMISSION

The actors have fifteen minutes in which to relax, repair their stage make-up and don their second act costumes, but the crew is busier than they have been during the act. Carpenters are dis-assembling the upstage wall unit and the dance hall set and storing them at the very back of the stage. They are not used at all in the second act. Likewise, the Properties crew is striking first act props and setting others, on stage and on the off-stage prop tables. David, the Assistant Stage Manager, is standing down stage center with his Intermission Check List, following the moves of the crew, available if there is a question. When the set-up is complete, he walks around the set, checks yet again to see if everything is where it should be, and walks over to the Stage Manager's desk to tell Ann that the stage is ready.

Richard has been filling out the Stage Manager's Nightly Report. It is given to the Producer's office after each performance, and includes the running times of each act, mention of any understudies who are performing, accidents, and any technical flaws in the production. Ann has gone to the dressing rooms, to check in with the actors. She notices the wardrobe woman hemming the leading lady's first scene skirt securely, watches the *Wig Dresser* putting the final hair pins into the leading lady's elaborate pompadour, and agrees to tell the Conductor that the leading man found the tempo too slow in his dance hall song. As she is leaving the dressing rooms, she hears Richard's voice on the intercom, calling "five minutes."

Above, actors may require several costume changes in a show, with accessories and makeup. Below, a wig dresser readies a wig of long hair. Photos: above NTC; below, R. Harden.

THE SECOND ACT

Back to the stage, a quick final check of the set and props, and into the sequence of calling the beginning of the second act; "places," House Lights, Curtains, Electrics, Sound, are called much like the opening of the show.

During the last big scene shift in the show, Ann looks up at a pipe flying in. Hanging from the pipe is a swag of heavy velvet curtain, edged with a wide gold fringe. A piece of the fringe has torn loose, and as she watches, it tangles around a light. "Flies," she calls over the headset, "You've got a foul stage right on the number sixteen batten."

"See it. Working on it." A moment passes. "It's not going to come loose, but it is still out of sight lines. Can we leave it where it is?" The curtain on the pipe cannot be seen by the audience yet, but because of the tangle of fringe, cannot be lowered to where it should be in the scene. The light cannot be used either.

"Leave it," says Ann. "Electrics? Take the specials on the fringed curtain out of the next cues, will you? We don't have a fringed curtain tonight."

"Right. Dimmer forty-five out of the rest of the cues." The light, without the curtain that it is aimed at, would be distracting to the audience. The rest of the shift is completed; the orchestra reprise of the music box theme heralds the last scene of the show; the lights come up, much as they did at the opening, on the actors listening to the music box.

During a lull in cue calling, after the start of the final song, Ann once again calls to Electrics. "The fifth light from the left on the number fourteen batten. Does it play again in the show tonight?"

"Just in the curtain call," is the answer.

"Better take it out," she says. The fringe from the curtain is caught around it, and I'd hate for it to start to smoke."

"Will do. The Flyman and I will look at it tonight. It'll be fixed to-morrow, so that it doesn't happen again."

One last sustained note hovers in the air. The lights slowly fade, the curtain falls to darkness and tumultous applause. On the headset, Ann calls "Curtain and bow light, GO." She calls the curtain down and up seven times. With the opening night audience, at least, we are a hit.

Although there are only two people in the cast, there are twenty-six of us backstage. Three Stage Managers, two Lighting Board Operators, two Floor Electricians, two Sound Operators, two Followspot Operators, two Properties people, three in the Flies, four Carpenters, two Dressers, a Wardrobe Mistress, a Wig Dresser and a House Crew of two. Depending on the advance ticket sales and the words of the drama critics in tomorrow's newspapers, we may be a part of a show that will run for years, or that will close tomorrow.

Meanwhile, we all finish up our workday. The Properties Mistress is washing dishes and storing the props away; sound and electrical gear is turned off; costumes are hung up. Notes are made about what has to be checked or repaired tomorrow. The Stage Manager's Nightly Report is completed.

The audience has left the theatre; the House Curtain is raised. The Electrician walks on stage with a stand about five feet tall, a single lit light bulb at its top. He sets it downstage center, the night light or "ghost" light.

The illumination from the ghost light is dim; we cannot really see the few pieces of scenery left on the stage. The theatre looks dark and empty, just as it looked two weeks ago, when we moved our company of actors and technicians, our truckloads of scenery, costumes and electrical gear into this space.

The depth of the house, and the action required on stage by the director and choreographer, are two major elements considered in set design.
Photos: NTC.

CHAPTER 2

GETTING IT DESIGNED

As we saw the ghost light placed on the stage tonight, and went up to our office to lock up the Prompt Script and get ready for the opening night party,we were struck by the loneliness of the deserted theatre. It was only two weeks ago that our show "loaded in" to this, then empty, theatre; only a few short months ago that the production began to take shape. Let's go back for a moment and look at the staff, designers, technicians and organization that brought this production to life.

Six months ago, our producer acquired the rights to produce this musical, not his first venture on Broadway. Before that, the composer and lyricist had played through several versions of the show for him. He had also seen a workshop production of it, a very minimal production, done for a short run in a small off-off Broadway theatre. The producer had reached a contractual agreement with the creators of this show: the Composer, Lyricist and Librettist, or book writer.

FINDING THE STAFF

The next people to be found were those responsible for translating the work from the printed page to the stage; the Director, Choreographer and Musical Director. All of the people who are a part of the project have extensive, accurate files of people with whom they have worked, or whose work they have seen and liked. The Composer and Librettist suggest a Director who had worked with them on a previous project. He is called, is sent a script, and the Composer and Librettist meet with him and play through some of the songs in the show. The Director is interested, becomes a part of the production team, and begins discussing the script and staging with the authors. The Composer suggests a Musical Director who has worked with him before. A Choreographer, who has done many shows for this Producer, is hired.

The next step was the Producer's call to us. Ann, with several Broadway shows to her credit, came to mind. She signed an Actor's Equity Association contract as Production Stage Manager. A search through her files led to interviews with possible Stage Managers; Richard and David, who had worked previously together, were contracted. Now this team could begin planning and scheduling the production.

At the same time that they were finding Stage Managers, the Producer and Director discussed the question of who should design the show. The authors were strongly in favor of the *Scenic Designer* who had worked with them on the workshop production almost a year ago. The Director was familiar with this Scenic Designer's work, and the Designer was, of course, a member of the union for theatrical designers, U.S.A., the United Scenic Artists. A copy of the script was dispatched to the Designer, who read it and met with the Producer and the Director. In discussing the work, they seemed to agree about the basic style of presentation. The Scenic Designer was anxious to work on the project, and was hired.

As with several of the staff already hired, knowing the right person again came into play. Scenic designers most often work very closely with lighting designers. Often a stage setting may be designed totally with lighting in mind. Lights can help finish the look of a play by setting the mood, the time, and even the location of a scene. In the Broadway hit *Dreamgirls,* a moveable pipe structure serving as a mounting position for the lights *was* the set. There is indeed a Lighting Designer who most often works with our Scenic Designer. Again, a script is sent, a meeting is arranged, all seems to be in agreement, and the Lighting Designer is hired.

We weren't so immediately lucky in finding a *Costume Designer.* Several people who were the choices of the Producer and the

Director were called. Unfortunately for us, but very fortunately for them, they were working on other projects. The young Designer who had done the workshop production was working on a film in Los Angeles, and therefore unavailable. Everyone's files were again consulted; the Designers who turned us down were asked for recommendations. One of them suggested a young man who had recently passed his union exam, and had just been working as the recommending Designer's assistant on a musical.

The interview process became a bit more formal in this case. None of the production staff was familiar with the young man's work, although all of us were impressed with the recommendation given him by the Designer that we did know. The Designer arrived at the Producer's office with a large artist's portfolio, a box of slides, and a portable slide projector. He gave a copy of his resume to the Producer, who realized that he had seen several examples of the young man's work in small off-off Broadway productions. The portfolio contained water color renderings of costumes which he had designed, and photographs of them as they looked on stage. The slides showed further examples of his work; the majority of clothes were from the latter part of the 19th and early 20th century, since he knew that to be the period in which our show is set. His work was very impressive. The Director was called to look at it, the Costume Designer was hired and given a script, and a date was set for a first meeting to discuss design concepts for our show.

THE FIRST PRODUCTION MEETING

Two weeks later, we all met in the Producer's office. The Producer, Director, Choreographer, Stage Managers, Scenic, Costume and Lighting Designers and the Authors are all on hand for this first discussion by the team. We are all on time, and the first of many pots of coffee is brewing. Sitting around the conference table, we resemble the executive meeting of a corporation; and in a way, we are, with the Producer the chairman of the board, the Director the President and the Stage Managers the chiefs of operations.

The purpose of this meeting is twofold: first to find out the facts of the production. The Producer tells us budget figures, dates, and what theatre we will likely play. The second purpose is for us, together, to find a common artistic track, to talk about *how* the Designers and Director are going to approach this script. We, as Stage Managers, begin one of our most important functions at this stage of production, which is to keep accurate records of all of the little details that are discussed.

The Producer starts things off by announcing which Broadway theatre he has contracted to house our show. There is general agreement that it is a good choice. It has a beautiful audience area that is intimate enough for a two character piece, and a more than adequate stage area. The designers are given budget allocations for each of their departments. The Producer announces the date that we will "load in" (move the scenery, lights and sound gear and costumes into the theatre and begin to set them up); a date less than a week later when we will have our first preview performance before an audience; and the opening date, which will occur after a full week of previews.

Ann has fastened a very large calendar to the wall of the conference room, and we begin to fill in dates and deadlines. Starting backwards, with the date that the scenery and electrical equipment must be ready to "load out" of the shops that will build or prepare them, we determine when the shops must have final designs or equipment lists, and when we will have further meetings to discuss and approve of the designs. Everyone copies the deadlines into their date books. Both Ann and the Producer emphasize how important it will be to keep to the schedule. Over a hundred people will be involved in getting this show on; the ten people at this meeting, the Producer's administrative and publicity staff, musicians, actors, the people who work in the various shops that will build and assemble the show, the crew who will run it. It is a complex people-machine that we are launching. Time lost can result in a great deal of money spent in overtime.

Now, the authors and the Director begin to give us all their impressions of how the show ought to look and feel. Our authors speak, in theatrical terms, about the two people they have created in their show. They are trying to encompass the lives of these two people over the course of many years. The characters have been many places, met many people, and been affected by many situations.

The Director emphasizes that parts of the musical are very realistic, while parts of it are seen in memory. The Composer plays a tape recording of the music box theme which occurs before each of the memory sections. The Director asks that the Scenic and Lighting Designers, particularly, provide a different "look" for the two sections. Everybody gets into a discussion of what memory looks like. The Designers are writing words like "soft," "fuzzy," "selective," and "honey-colored" on their pads. Then, more specifically, the Director goes through the scenes of the musical, giving us as much information as he can about where scenes happen, and how much of the stage area he envisions will be needed, while still using an abstract language that may spark the Designers' thinking. "Act Two, scene three," he says, "will probably not take place on the *Titanic,* but on any ocean liner."

"Good," replies the Scenic Designer, "I have to give you an ocean, but no iceburg." The ocean waves and bit of ship's rail that he doodles in the margin of his pad will become the germ of the set for that scene.

The Costume Designer points out that the leading lady should be in the same dress in the three scenes that take place before the birth of the couple's children. That way, in Act Two, when our star pulls that dress from her trunk, the audience will know that she is reminiscing about her children. He also makes a note that he will have to provide duplicates of that dress as the prop for the trunk. The Choreographer points out that the dress, despite the heavy look of the period, must be very easy to handle and move in; our star's most strenuous dancing will be done in one of those scenes.

The meeting goes on, frequently jumping from specifics to the abstract. We all feel that a good beginning has taken place; the Designers are anxious to get to their drawing boards. Richard pours the last cup from the fifth pot of coffee as Ann reaches accord with everyone as to when the next meetings between Director and Designers will take place.

THE SCENIC DESIGNER

Back in his studio, the Scenic Designer is re-reading the latest version of the script for about the fifth time. Each time he reads, it is with a different purpose in mind. His earlier readings were to get an impression of the overall work, to see what happens, to begin to formulate his responses to its structure in line and color. Now, with the meeting over, he reads for specific information. How many scenes are there which require different sets? He makes a note to ask the Director if the dining room and living room interiors could be combined into one set which repeats in the two scenes. How many entrances (doors and archways) must each set have? Which are the "real" scenes and which the "memory" scenes?

He finds a note from the meeting saying that Act One, scene eight should be "green." Just what exactly does that mean? The scene takes place in mid-town New York in 1929. Perhaps "green" has something to do with the sickness that was felt after the Stock Market crash. How can he translate that note into a stage setting that will convey that impression to an audience?

The Designer realizes that it is important for him to find out just exactly what offices really looked like in New York in 1929. Not that he intends faithfully to reconstruct one; this is a musical, and one of the "memory" parts of the show. But as background, and a starting-off place, some research on the Depression is in order. This is a perfect job for his assistant. A Designer's assistant does all sorts of jobs that leave the Designer more time for purely creative thinking about the play. In addition to research, the Assistant may do some drafting, search out and price special materials, look for furniture and other stage properties, and keep track of shop schedules. The Assistant has been hired by the Producer, at the Designer's request.

A phone call, and the Designer's assistant is off to the library, to search out and scan picture books of the period. He calls the local historical society, to see if they have any material that might be of help, and discovers from them that there is a specialized picture collection held by an architectural association. The next day he is back at work, this time seeking out pictures of luxury ocean liners of the period.

As the Scenic Designer studies this material, and thumbs through the script again and again, he begins preliminary sketches for the show. His first sketches are for himself. They are pictures of how he sees the show "in a perfect world," if the size of the theatre and the size of the budget were not considerations. From these idealized "dream" designs, tempered by the realities of time, space, money and the demands of the Director and the other Designers, will come the settings for the show.

Since the Designer is trained to think in terms of pictures, he will probably do many small, "thumbnail" pencil sketches. Some of these are nothing more than experiments with the basic sizes and shapes of the various settings, his method of "doodling." They will also provide a convenient and efficient way of communicating with the Director when they next meet. And indeed, before he commits his overall design scheme to paper, he will meet with the Director. The Designer's assistant and a Stage Manager will be present to take notes. Is this what the Director had in mind? Should this effect be more pronounced? More distorted? They may begin to discuss color.

Back at the drawing board, reality begins to set in for our Scenic Designer. He has a full set of plans for the theatre we will be in, and the latest script changes have been given to him. Scene by scene, he develops the show's *ground plan*. A ground plan shows graphically the arrangement of the scene on the stage floor, the position of all items of scenery and furniture, the entrances and exits, the extent and height of all levels, the position and size of all steps, open traps and ramps. He checks the plans of the theatre to make sure that his scenery will fit into the space provided. He double checks the script to see that he has supplied all of the necessary doors, windows and furnishings that it demands.

At last he can begin to do some rough sketches of what the show will look like. In just a few days, he has another appointment with the Director. At this meeting he must have as many visual aids as possible to help the Director see what the Designer is trying to achieve. The Designer will do several sketches to show each set for each scene, so it can be understood. Once again, these are merely in black and white—pencil sketches on sketch paper. At this point, the Designer simply wants to see if he understands the type of look that the Director has in mind. He would rather get details of shape and mass settled before adding color.

Our set is very complicated. It has several large pieces of scenery which move together in a variety of ways. The Designer will bring a model to the next meeting, in addition to his drawings. The model combines the pictorial nature of the sketch with the precise factual character of the ground plan. It is a three-dimensional representation of the set, to ¼-inch scale, showing the skeletal structure of the house for the "memory" scenes, and the real walls that fill in or play in front of this skeleton. Again, it is white, constructed from light-weight cardboard.

Scenic models have become very popular. It is difficult for someone who is not a designer to be able to visualize walls from the two dimensions of a ground plan, or to determine accurately from a perspective drawing the amount of actual space available for actors. It is a very useful device in plotting the movement pattern of the scenic pieces as they are shifted from one scene to another. The Director may wish to plot complicated moves on it, using it like a chess board for actors. The model may remain the simple "white model" the Designer has taken with him today; it may have color, furniture and detail added until it becomes a doll house miniature of the finished set.

At their next meeting, using the model, the Designer shows the Director his concept for the entire show, the look of each scene, and how the scenery changes from one scene to the next. The Director may suggest changes; further alterations may become necessary because of script re-writes. Slowly, these two people will come to agreement on the look of the scenes and of the overall show.

In collaboration with the Costume and Lighting Designers, who are present at this meeting, color is discussed. A "palette," or range of colors is determined, then colors for specific scenes. The "memory" parts of the show will feature soft "earth" colors; golds, ambers, browns and a greyed green. The "real" parts of the show will be brighter, but similar colors: red, yellow, dark green, and a great deal of polished brown and yellow-brown wood. The Costume Designer has brought swatches of fabrics in the colors that earlier discussions had led him to think about; the Lighting Designer has a swatch book of colored gels. A general consensus is reached; lavender and purple will be used only as occasional accents and for the leading lady's dance hall dress; blue for the dress in the trunk. The Lighting Designer, now knowing what colors her lights will be focused upon, can determine her own palette of gels. And she is thinking how to achieve the look of a "soft, out-of-focus, sepia photograph," one of the descriptive phrases from the meeting, which she finds challenging, but helpful. The Costume Designer departs with a firm idea of the set colors, including some paint swatches, an envelope of fabric swatches labelled "try to avoid these colors" and another envelope labelled "look for this sort of thing." Only a few of the decisions are firm and precise at this point, but all three of the Designers and the Director are beginning to share a way of looking at the show.

The Scenic Designer returns to his studio. He incorporates any changes into his sketches, his ground plan and his model. He prepares color sketches of the sets for the different scenes as an aid to further discussion with the Director and the other Designers. For the larger sets which they have already discussed in great detail, and on which they seem to have reached an agreement, he may prepare a watercolor rendering, in perspective and quarter inch scale. He may, instead, apply color and detail to the model.

But about this time there is another deadline marked on his wall calendar. He must have drawings and materials ready to submit to the scene shops which will be submitting bids to build and paint the set. Ultimately, the Scenic Designer is responsible for detailed construction drawings of how each part of the set is to be built; these drawings also specify materials. Not all of this is completed when he first meets with the shop Manager; the shop people are very likely to have ideas about materials and methods that will be cheaper and faster. Nevertheless, for several days, the Scenic Designer and his assistant are bending over drawing boards, manipulating scale rulers and templates, and consulting hardware catalogs, fabric swatches, moulding catalogs and seeking out plastics manufacturers. They become very grateful for the presence of their electric pencil sharpener and electric eraser.

THE DESIGN STUDIO

Across town, in a studio somewhat similar to the Scenic Designer's, the Costume Designer has for weeks been going through a somewhat similar process. Both studios, not surprisingly, look like artist's workspaces. There are shelves of picture books; collections of photographs and paintings from historical periods from ancient Greece to the present day. As well as a drafting table, the studios are stocked with a range of artist's materials—pastels, felt markers, tempera paints, dyes, inks, brushes, drawing pencils and pens, an airbrush. The Scenic Designer, who is a serious model maker, stocks a collection of woods and veneers, a small electric saw and a model-maker's small lathe and chisels. The Costume Designer, who is likely to want to experiment with the drape of a fabric or the cut of a sleeve has both a sewing machine and a dressmaker's form at hand, and a convenient deep sink to test samples of dye. Both are likely to have an electric hair blow-drier hanging by a work table; it is convenient for quickly drying paint and dye samples. Their spaces are well lighted; the lights probably include one or more stage lighting fixtures, into which they can insert lighting color media (gels) to test the look of their work under various colors of light. Each Designer provides his or her own working space; they do not move their studios from show to show. Some Designer's studios are in or adjacent to their homes, some have totally separate living and working spaces.

THE COSTUME DESIGNER

The Costume Designer has also read the play many times. The margins of his script are covered with notes, dates and quick sketches. For this show, he has turned the pages of dozens of books, looking at pictures of both high fashions and ordinary clothes from 1880 to 1930, the years encompassed by the script. He has also looked, in books and at museums, at paintings of the French Impressionists, since the Director mentioned this as a kind of look he was seeking in the "memory" sections. He has also studied the works of Expressionist painter Edward Munch, which are of the proper period, and seem to have a sharp sense of the society in which they were painted that seems right for the "real" parts of the show. His assistant has gone to the library and picture collections seeking out books of sepia "art photos" from the twenties; the Designer and the assistant have examined authentic garments in several museum collections. The Costume Designer has made a number of sketches, some of complete costumes, some of details. There is a tower of books on his work table with book marks protruding from them.

Although there was a time in the theatre when actors were responsible for supplying their own clothes, and although this may still happen in modern dress shows in some school and community theatre productions, in the professional theatre, the Costume Designer is responsible for dressing the actors every time they are on stage. It is a rule of Actors' Equity Association, the actors' union, that the Producer must furnish their costumes.

The work of the Costume Designer which we have described above, to a great extent mirrors that of the Scenic Designer. Both have their ideas about the show influenced by the demands of the script and the interpretation of the Director; both engage in research on the background and look of the period in which the show takes place; both work from preliminary sketches to final drawings from which a set or a costume can be built; for both this involves a string of meetings, first with the Director and the other Designers, later with the construction shops.

An additional aspect of the Costume Designer's job makes it one of the most difficult in the theatre. The Scenic and Lighting Designers work with given spaces and mainly with inanimate objects. The set must be safe for the actors to work on; costumes, however, are things that, on stage, actors truly live in. They are an extention of the character that the actor has created. The Costume Designer is working with vital, constantly changing human beings, both actors and characters. Every person has feelings about the way he or she looks. Actors on stage in front of a thousand people have very definite ideas and prejudices about their appearance. The Costume Designer must be aware of these human feelings and incorporate them into the designs. It requires a sharp eye and a great deal of tact.

For his first meeting with the Director after the initial Production Meeting, the Costume Designer will bring a few sketches, but not of all of the costumes for all of the characters. For some scenes, he may provide several different looks, so that the Director may choose, or simply to help clarify the discussion of what the costume should be. For this show, our Costume Designer is fortunate; it is cast long before rehearsals start. He knows what the performers whom he is dressing look like, and can design the costumes for their particular shapes and coloring.

He continues to go back and forth between the script and his research, finding in the script details of plot and character which determine the specific look of each costume, finding many examples of that kind of costume, gradually choosing and creating exactly the right one. There is a 1920's dance hall scene. Is the dance hall elegant or wild or casual? Is the character shy or brazen? Did she buy or make the dress herself, or was it supplied to her by the owners of the dance hall? Is she comfortable in the dance hall, or does she want to be somewhere else? Answers are found, designs emerge and change upon discussion with the Director and the other Designers. It is possible that all of the designs may change as the script is re-written. Such is the excitement and heartbreak of an original production.

Like the Scenic Designer's early sketches, the Costume Designer's first work is in black and white. After the meeting with the Director and the other Designers in which color was discussed (and there was some mention of fabrics), the Costume Designer makes final sketches. They may be color renderings, done in water color, pastels, felt marker or airbrush inks; they may be ink or pencil sketches, with suggested fabrics attached. Most important, they are drawn in such a way that the look of the costume is very clear; it is from this sketch that a cutter in the costume shop must draft the pattern from which the costume will be constructed. Fabric swatches are often attached to the sketch at this point. The costume shop will not be able to duplicate this fabric in all cases, but the swatches provide them, and provide the Director, with a clear idea of what the actors will be wearing.

The costume designs are also shown to the actors. It will help them as they rehearse, to know what they will be wearing in each scene. They may want to simulate some pieces of costume in rehearsals; a long skirt, a scarf for the feather boa, a vest that has to be taken off and then put on again. The actors will have ideas about what looks well on them, and about what their characters would wear. Without losing control of the design, the Costume Designer listens to their ideas, and tries to incorporate whichever ones are possible. If an actor feels that he or she looks bad on stage, looks "out of character," that actor will not perform well. The design process, at this stage, calls into play discussion, tact, diplomacy and often a bit of flattery.

Armed with final sketches and swatches, the Costume Designer goes off to a meeting with the Director, the final one before the designs are submitted to the shops. But there has been another script change. The actress now has a maximum of only twenty seconds between scenes four and five of Act One in which to completely change her costume. The looks of both costumes are exactly right as they are, but alterations must be made in the way in which they are constructed so that our leading lady, aided by a very efficient dresser, can change from one outfit to the other in that short amount of time.

The costume sketches are submitted to several shops, for bids on the cost of supplying them. The manager of the shop reviews them with the Costume Designer, determining types and amounts of fabric and trim, and the amount of labor involved in building each one. Similar to the manager of the scenic shop, the costume shop manager may have suggestions about economical changes that can be made in choice of fabric or patterning.

The bulk of the creative work of the Scenic Designer and the Costume Designer is done at their drawing boards. They will be very busy through the rest of the production process, and it is very likely that changes in the script and direction will make it necessary for them to make alterations in their designs. But for the most part, the rest of their work is finishing details and solving problems as they arise. The Lighting Designer, on the other hand, has a great deal of preparation to do, but the bulk of her creative work will happen in the theatre, as she determines the lighting of each scene.

THE LIGHTING DESIGNER

The Lighting Designer, if you remember, was at the first Production Meeting. She took careful notes as the authors and the Director discussed their ideas about the play. At times she asked questions to clarify the time of day and the general mood of individual scenes. Returning to her studio, which contains a large drafting table and a comprehensive collection of catalogs of stage lighting and electrical equipment, she, like the other designers, reads and re-reads the script. Before she can start to draft her lighting plot, though, she needs some information from the Scenic Designer. She must have some indication of the shape and size of the sets that she will be lighting; and only when she knows where scenery will be hanging can she determine the placement of her lights.

In going over the script, she makes notes of any *practicals,* such as table lamps, street lights, fixtures that must light up on the stage, seemingly controlled by the actors. She lists any effects that she will be responsible for, such as the twinkling stars in the summer night scene, and begins to think of possible ways to build them. Projections are going to be used on a curtain in Act One. What should they look like? She obtains a print of the theatre that we are going into, and perhaps, if she has never done a show there, visits it to look at the places in the front of the house from which lights may be hung. Does this theatre pose any difficult problems? What particular size and wattage of lighting unit will best light the stage from the house lighting positions?

Although there have been Broadway shows such as *Candide* and *Cats* which completely restructured the audience area, this is relatively rare. In most Broadway theatres, lights can be placed on the fronts of one or two balconies, sometimes in a cove in the ceiling or a pipe suspended from it, and often on tall pipe stands, called "booms" in the house boxes. The Lighting Designer becomes familiar with the space she will be working in, and with the demands of the show she will be lighting.

As soon as she has a ground plan and a *hanging plot* (an indication of what pieces of scenery and curtains will hang from what pipe) from the Scenic Designer, she can begin her preliminary work. On

Dorothy Loudon leads dancers in rehearsal for a major New York
production. Photo: Camera 1, New York.

a ground plan of the full stage, with all of the sets indicated, she will mark each pipe and boom to which lights will be attached, and indicate their heights. This is the beginning of the *light plot*, which also will contain a scale outline (usually half-inch scale) of each light. Neatly lettered numbers or symbols indicate the specific type of lighting unit, the color of its gel, and whether it is plugged together with any other instruments.

The Lighting Designer's first duty is to light the actors, to make the play visible to the audience. She is also aware of light as it determines weather or time of day; of the differences between indoor and outdoor lighting; of the uses of light to enhance the scenery and to elicit a mood for the scene. She plans to achieve the "memory" look by the use of several shades of amber and pale brown-reds that will not be used in the other parts of the show, and by using very strong *backlight,* light from behind the actors.

She translates these ideas and visions into equipment, calling upon a great deal of experience with all of the various types of stage lighting instruments, and making sure to request even more equipment than she thinks will be needed. Some decisions about the set may not have been made by the time the lighting equipment list must be submitted to the lighting shop; there are likely to be changes in the script and in the direction which will necessitate changes in the lighting. Although additional equipment can be procured and hung after the show is set up in the theatre, this is costly in both money and person-hours.

The Lighting Designer calls Ann and Richard and insists on coming to a run-through of as much of the play as is ready as soon as she can. Only by seeing the actors move in space can she come to final decisions about what the light must look like, where it must be, when it must be brighter, when dimmer, and how the lights will flow from scene to scene.

The Lighting Designer, too, has an assistant, who may help her with preliminary drafting and list making. The bulk of the assistant's work will be record-keeping and helping in the theatre, when the Designer is actually writing the "cues" for the show; when she is "painting with light" what the audience will see.

Certainly questions will arise, and the Stage Managers or the

Director will have to be called. They, in turn, take care to keep the Lighting Designer informed of changes in the script or the scenic design which may affect the lighting design. The meeting at which color was discussed was very important for the Lighting Designer. She made a point of looking very carefully at the fabric swatches of the Costume Designer, taking some of them with her so she could look at them under various colors of gel. She probably does not, however, go through lengthy discussions of her work with the Director. She cannot draw sketches of how lights will look; the Director's contributions to her work will come in the theatre, during technical rehearsals.

Once the lighting plot is complete, the Lighting Designer prepares an equipment list. This lists, pipe by pipe and boom by boom, all of the equipment that she wishes to rent in order to light the show. It includes not only the lighting instruments, but the pipes themselves, the heavy bases for the booms, the hardware that will attach the light to the pipe, and the cable that will connect the light to the control board. The equipment list also describes the number and type of controllers that the light board is to contain. The list specifies the type and quantity of follow spots. From this list, the lighting rental shops will determine their bid for a rental price for the equipment.

Devices used in the lighting of the show that the lighting rental shop does not have on their shelves, but must purchase or build to order, will be purchased by the producer. At the same time that the equipment list is submitted, the Lighting Designer sends the shop detailed drawings of any such "specials." The twinkling lights in the summer night scene are an example.

THE SOUND DESIGNER

The *Sound Designer* may or may not have been at our first Production Meeting, but he will soon be at work. His work is really divided into two parts: program sound, or sound effects, and sound reinforcement. He starts his work with the script and the score.

In determining the sound effects, he first, of course, reads the script from which he soon compiles a list of the barking dog, the steam engine, the boat horns, etc. Do they really want crickets in the summer night scene? And what about the music box? It is time to meet with the Director and the Stage Managers. They decide on the sounds needed, and begin to talk about what they should be like. The dog should not sound vicious; the steam engine and the boat horn are in the "memory" sections, and should have that quality. Should there be other ocean sounds during the boat scene? Seagulls? Perhaps. Not necessarily crickets for the summer evening, but some sort of night sounds. Peepers? A clock in the distance, striking nine? The music box theme will be played by the orchestra many times, with different instrumentation, but the first and last times it is heard, it will be on tape, and must sound as though it is being played by the prop music box on stage. This is something to be discussed with the Musical Director.

The Sound Designer begins to find and make sounds. Some of them he may have in his collection of tapes; copies of some of them can be purchased from a number of sound studios; the New York street noises and the boat horns, he may tape himself. As soon as he has a representative collection, he will play some of them for the Director and the Stage Managers. They will decide which exactly is the right, un-menacing barking dog. In recording them, he will filter and distort the "memory" sounds to secure the proper effect.

In his meeting with the Director, the Sound Designer has also determined from what direction the various sounds must come. The boat horns come from stage left, but the other "memory" sounds surround the audience. Can a speaker be built into the hassock which the actors sit near when they play the music box? This is a question to be cleared with the Scenic Designer. Yes, it can, and there is a way to conceal the connecting cable, and to strike it during the scene shift. But it means that the hassock must be built, rather than purchased or rented. Is the effect worth the expense? It is an important moment of the show. The Producer decides that it is worth it.

Gradually, the Sound Designer determines approximate positions for all of the speakers and checks this with the Scenic Designer; both adjust and make compromises. He is beginning to assemble an equipment list of the playback equipment, amplifiers, speakers and control equipment that will be needed.

The other major responsibility of the sound designer, that of sound reinforcement, involves decisions about the sound of the orchestra. After discussions with the composer on the nature of the sound that he has in mind, and further discussions with the Musical Director and the Arranger, the Sound Designer must determine all of the equipment to get the best sound possible to the audience. He will concern himself with the balance of the electric bass and the acoustic piano. He will decide how many, what type, and where to put any microphones for the actors. He will decide on the wireless microphones, or "body mikes" to be used in certain scenes. Like the Lighting Designer, a good deal of the Sound Designer's work will be done when the equipment is set up in the theatre. Sound is affected by its surroundings to a tremendous extent. The Sound Designer must make decisions based upon knowledge of the effect of sound in the closed space of the Scenic Designer's setting. Also like the Lighting Designer, the Sound Designer must call upon his knowledge of available equipment to begin his work. The most creative time for the Sound and Lighting Designers is toward the opening of the show, when the Costume and Scenic Designers are nearing the completion of their work.

The Sound Designer's plot is a detailed diagram of the ways in which the various pieces of equipment which he has specified will be connected. He, too, prepares an equipment list for submittal to a sound shop. It lists each piece of equipment, specifying type and usually manufacturer, the length of each speaker and microphone cable, and the type of connector. The sound shops will prepare a bid on the cost of renting this equipment.

GETTING DESIGNS TO THE SHOPS

During the weeks that all of these people have been working, we, the Stage Managers, have been in constant contact with them. We have helped to keep them apprised of changes in the script and the music. We must now gently remind them how close we are to loading into the theatre, and to opening. It is time for the Designers to push their ideas into realities.

From preliminary drawings, several scenic shops and costume shops have presented bids. A time of negotiation has gone on. For reasons of cost, some changes have been made in the designs; for reasons of both cost and efficiency, the shops have suggested other changes in materials and construction methods. The Producer has selected the shops who will build the shows. The Scenic Designer must supply the scene shop with complete working drawings and detailed painters' elevations for the painting to be done on all drops and scenery. He or his assistant will phone and visit the shops as the work proceeds. The Costume Designer has also submitted final sketches. He, too, and his assistant will be looking at the shop's progress, making decisions about finishing and trim, and helping to seek out materials.

Likewise, several sound and lighting shops have submitted bids on the equipment lists submitted to them. There has been a negotiating process, and the designers may have decreased the amount of equipment that they have requested, for reasons of cost. The shops have been selected, and the Electricians and Sound Operators for the show are preparing to go to work at these shops, assembling their equipment.

A WORD ABOUT ASSISTANTS

We have mentioned that the assistants to the Scenic and Costume Designers have been hard at work during this stage of the design process. The assistants to the Lighting and Sound Designers are somewhat involved in this part of the work; they will be kept very busy once we start technical rehearsals. Design assistant is a journeyman position. Scenic, Costume and Lighting Design assistants must be members of United Scenic Artists, the Designer's union. They are often young Designers, learning the working details of their chosen profession.

While the creative thinking and exchange of ideas between Directors and Designers is taking place, many routine design tasks are done by assistants. Someone must investigate the library and other research sources. Someone must begin making up equipment lists for shop orders. Someone must build the model which the Director will finally approve. Assistants relieve the Designer, who may be working on more than one show at a time, of necessary chores, all the while they are observing the process that is going on and learning from it. An assistant's duties will vary from Designer to Designer and from show to show, basically doing whatever the Designer needs done in order to complete the job.

As work begins in the shops, assistants will undertake even more important functions. It will probably be the Scenic Designer's assistant who will check, each day, on the progress of the building and painting. The assistant did much of the drafting that went to the shop, and will know the workings of the set, inside and out.

The Costume Designer's assistant probably helped to locate many of the fabrics being used and will know if and where more can be found. The costume assistant will also be of great help during the preliminary fittings; having worked closely with the Designer from the beginning, the assistant will speak the Designer's language, understand the design concept, and will be asked to solve problems all through the process.

At this stage of the design process, in the preparation of the equipment list, and to a greater extent once they begin to work in the theatre, the Lighting Designer's assistant will function as organizer. The world of lighting is one of numbers, charts and records. There will come a time when the Designer must look up at the stage, intent upon the movements of the actors and the look of the lights. Someone must look down at the paper and record the vision that the Designer is creating. That someone is the assistants.

The relationship between Designer and assistant is symbiotic. Most assistants are young designers in their own right, but the world of the theatre is often difficult to crack into. In addition to experience, the assistant gains valuable exposure in this closed world. Producers, Directors and other Designers become acquainted with his or her abilities. Soon the assistants will be hiring their own assistants.

Meanwhile, at the rehearsal hall, and soon at shops all over town, we are getting a show together.

Costume shop manager Hilary Sherred describes to shopper Karen
Henriksen the materials she must try to locate in New York shops such as
the accessories store above. Photos: R. Harden.

CHAPTER 3

GETTING IT ORGANIZED

After preliminary design decisions are made by the creative staff, we begin the process of turning these ideas into sets and costumes and props—into a production. As Stage Managers, we are a pivotal part of this process, responsible for having at our fingertips a knowledge of decisions that have been made, changes that are being made, and everybody's phone number.

Geographically, we expand a great deal. Although there are still occasional small meetings in a studio, office or living room, rehearsals are taking place in one or more rented spaces in the city; the costumes are to be built in one or more of the shops in town; the lighting equipment is to be gathered together and labeled somewhere else; another shop is working on the heavy stage machinery, the electric or hydraulic gear that moves the more massive pieces of scenery; the set is being constructed in yet another shop; the Designer's assistants and prop people are hunting down curtains and bric-a-brac and pictures for the walls (known as *set dressing*), furniture (*set props*), and keeping lists of the dishes, notebooks, briefcases, drinking glasses and reading glasses that the actors must handle (*hand props*). The Producer has a mid-town office, from which the financial and promotional details of the production are handled, and we sometimes work from there, but since at least one of us must be present at each rehearsal, a great deal of our work seems to be done from pay phones throughout the city. We all carry a great many dimes.

41

GETTING THE ACTORS TOGETHER

While the physical part of the production is beginning to become a reality, of course the Director has cast the show and has begun rehearsing with the actors. And as Stage Managers, we are very much involved in this aspect of production. First the actors must be chosen. The process of auditioning and casting begins. Although the male star of this show was decided on at the very beginning, the female star was not. Actors' agents are called, reading copies of the script are sent out, and meetings are held. Since this is such a small cast, the Producer and the Director do most of the interviewing and the dealing with agents and performers, but the Stage Management staff must keep the records. We file pictures and resumes of all of the actors seen. Their phone numbers, answering service phone numbers and their agent's phone number all find a place in the first of the many notebooks that we will fill up with lists.

And, in addition to our two cast members, we must have a stand-by for each of them—performers who will be at the theatre each night, ready to go on stage should the regular actor be unable to come to the theatre, or become ill during the performance. The actors' union, Actors' Equity Association, requires that we hold Equity Principal Interviews (known as E.P.I.s) for any production done on Broadway. These interviews usually take place on two consecutive days, either in a rehearsal studio or in a room at the Actor's Equity Association headquarters. The Director is present, and the Producer may be. One of us helps the union monitor organize the actors waiting to be seen, giving out numbers so that they may be seen in some order, and answering whatever questions the actors may have. The actor talks briefly with the Director and Producer and leaves a "picture and resume," an 8″ x 10″ glossy photograph and a one page listing of their theatrical experience, education and roles they have played. Another one of us, in the interviewing room, keeps track of the pictures and resumes, perhaps making marginal notes on them, so that we will have a chance of remembering the several hundred people that we will see each day. We may find someone whom we wish to ask to come back and audition for the woman's role or we may find someone whom we wish to have audition as a stand-by.

And although there are only two people in our show, the manilla folder of pictures and resumes of "possible" actors becomes rather fat—we may lose a cast member or a stand-by; and should the show be a hit, there will be a need for replacements and casts for a road company. We may as well get some of this work done ahead of time.

At the end of each exhausting day, we review things with the Director and Producer, and then set about arranging auditions for those people whom we are seriously considering for roles. To the list of people from the E.P.I.s is added names submitted by agents. A Casting Director may be hired by the Producer, and may be helping with this process. Auditions are held, the business parts of the arrangements are seen to by the Producer and the General Manager, and eventually contracts are signed and we have a cast. As Stage Managers, we are also covered by contracts through the actor's union, but our contracts start two weeks before rehearsals begin, since by that time we are very busy co-ordinating meetings, arranging auditions, finding questions to ask and problems to solve.

THE STAGE MANAGER'S DUTIES IN REHEARSAL

At the first rehearsal, we oversee the union business of filling out insurance forms, holding the election for the company's union deputy and collecting W-4 forms and whatever other information the Producer may need. Often the Scenic and Costume designers are in attendance, briefly, at this first rehearsal, to meet the company, and to display the costume sketches and the set model, to hear the Director describe their joint approach to the production, and to begin to get to know the people with whom they will be working very closely for the next six weeks, and perhaps much longer.

We rehearse for eight hours a day, six days a week. One of the Stage Managers, but more often two, are always at rehearsals. There are certain union regulations, involving brief rest breaks and meal breaks that we must enforce. We begin the habit of calling the time each day to double check our watches. We keep track of the hours that each rehearsal lasts.

Most of our time at rehearsals is spent in the preparation of the

Prompt Script, that fat three-ring notebook that you saw us take out of the file drawer on opening night. This is an accurate record of the words, movements and technical happenings in the show. Before the first rehearsal, we have, perhaps with the help of the Designer's assistant, taped an indication of the set's floor plan on the floor of the rehearsal hall, or, if we are to be rehearsing in several different places, on a large canvas ground cloth that can be moved from place to place. We very carefully copy the Designer's ground plan onto the floor or cloth, using colored cloth or plastic tape. If there are several sets in the show, and there are in this one, each is taped in a different color. With the Director, we explain this layout to the actors—where the walls, doors, windows and bookcases are. As the actors start moving about, we try to keep an eye out that they don't walk through walls, something all too easy to do when their set has only two dimensions. As entrances, exits and movements are set, we make careful note of them in the prompt script, using both words and diagrams. We may mark words that are emphasized and make note of actors' motivations, because we are responsible for rehearsing the stand-bys, and will hold rehearsals for cast replacements. One of us may even direct the road company, if the show tours after its Broadway run.

We are certain that we make notes about anything that may affect the technical running of the show. Does someone turn on a light? Is a prop added? How big must that book be? What foods are the actors allergic to? What foods do they prefer? If you remember back to opening night, the Scotch whisky was made from apple juice, rather than cold tea or food coloring and water. How big should the plant that he brings her in the second scene be? What kind of a plant should it be? Is it important that we have several plants of different sizes so that it can appear to grow as the years seemingly pass? Do we have to call a botanist for help? Some of these questions have already been anticipated by the Designers from the script, some of them perhaps answered. But many of these details cannot be answered until the show begins to get "on its feet," until the Director and the actors begin making decisions and discoveries in the script.

Some of the markings in our Prompt Script concern the running of the show—when light cues happen, when scenery moves, when

The set may begin to take form in a drawing or a model like that of designer Jack Stewart's above. Then the plan is carried out in a shop like Hudson Scenic Studios; where the shop foreman, a carpenter, and the designer's assistant are going over plans, below. Photos: R. Harden.

sound effects happen. We will go over these cues with the Lighting and Sound Designers and with the Carpenter or Technical Director. Some information must immediately be communicated to the Designers, and passed on by them to the shops that are working on the show.

A bit of "stage business" evolves in a rehearsal: our leading lady must have a handkerchief. Is there a pocket in her dress? There should be. Check with the Costume Designer. If the leading lady exits on stage right and re-enters in the next scene from stage left, there will be less time for her costume change. Can it be done that quickly? If not, how can the costume be restructured to make it possible? Will she have to *underdress* (wear one costume underneath the other) so that the only change involved will be removing the first costume?

The Director decides that it is important that there be some kind of night sounds at the beginning of scene three to establish the fact that we are now in a peaceful countryside. This necessitates a call to the Sound Designer. Perhaps we can act as go-between for his discussion of kinds of sounds. Certainly with the help of the stopwatches that are either around our necks, or in our pockets, we can tell him if we anticipate 30 seconds of crickets or 10 minutes. He'll likely come prepared with twice what we ask for anyway.

It seems to make sense that the actress starts singing that song about dawn from the upstage window, rather than from the one stage right, which was where we had told the Lighting Designer it would happen. Call the Lighting Designer. Can she make the sun rise upstage as easily? Only if the Scenic Designer can add some bushes or something outside the window to *mask* (hide) the necessary lights. Call the Scenic Designer. Keep after both of them until we find the answer.

The little dance that the actors do when they get home from the party seems to want to take up more space than has been allotted on a platform. Can the platform be made bigger? The Scenic Designer had better stop by to discuss this with the Director. Is that part of the scenery built yet? How much will it cost to make the change? The Producer will have to get involved in this change if it is expensive.

Although the actors' primary job at this time is rehearsing, there are other demands on their time. They must make an appearance at the costume shop to be measured, and then to be fitted with their costumes. The trick mechanism that turns the ugly brass vase that she is polishing into a bouquet of red roses for the dream ballet is ready to be tried out. We take some rehearsal time for her to learn to work with it. The Publicist has requests for radio interviews to be taped at the radio stations and for pictures of rehearsal for the newspapers. Perhaps a television news program will want to come to a rehearsal to tape a feature. All of this must be scheduled by us, in such a way as to lose as little rehearsal time as possible.

And with all this, there are changes. There are always changes. It seems as though only opening night will see an end to the changes. A new play is evolving; quite a different matter from a revival, or a college or community theatre production of a play that has been done before. Some nights after rehearsals, the discussions between the Playwright, Director and Producer seem endless. Many mornings, rehearsals begin with a new scene or a re-written scene being presented to us. Most of the time, the Producer's administrative assistant or production secretary will provide us with copies of new scenes, although we have been known to type them ourselves, when inspiration strikes in the middle of a meeting.

We must make sure that the actors and the Director have copies of the changes. If they are substantive, if an entire scene is cut or added, we must get the corrected version to the Designers, since the changes are likely to affect their work. Perhaps we should telephone them and tell them about the change, then mail a copy to them. Most important, the change must be put into our Prompt Script. We indicate the date on the top of the page. We also date the pages that have been cut, and save them, in order, in another notebook. Some things that get cut one day will be restored the next, and we are responsible for having an accurate copy, perhaps the only copy, of the script at all times. And always, some corner of our collective heads must try to be aware of how any changes or re-writes affect any of the technical elements of the production. Must the costume change be faster? The sound cue deleted? The pool of light warm rather than cool? Must a prop be added? We make notes throughout rehearsals, discuss them with the Director, and transmit information to the Designers.

When the lighting units have been prepared for use by the shop electricians, the show electrician marks and packs them. Photo: R. Harden.

CHAPTER 4

GETTING IT BUILT

ABOUT THEATRICAL SHOPS

Early in the twentieth century, in the heyday of lavish revues and huge cast musicals (*Desert Song, The Red Mill, The Student Prince*), each producing organization not only employed a full time staff of technicians, but also owned and operated their own shops in which scenery, props, costumes and lighting effects and equipment were built, stored and maintained. A combination of fewer productions, higher salaries for theatre workers and enormously high real estate costs for the vast amounts of space needed for shops and storage have made this kind of organization obsolete. A handful of shops, combined with a collection of craftspeople and consultants, build and prepare almost all Broadway shows. Perhaps only the shop foreman and an apprentice or two are guaranteed full-time employment; all other workers are hired as they are required. In practice, a dozen or more persons are kept busy in each of the shops; the number can double during a busy part of a season, but can fall back to a bare minimum as work tapers off. Many Stage Carpenters and Electricians normally hold down two jobs— working on a show evenings and matinees, and in a shop daytimes.

It is necessary that scenery for a Broadway show be built in a "Union Shop", a scenic studio under the jurisdiction of the International Alliance of Theatrical Stage Employees (IATSE or IA). Scene painting must be done by a member of the United Scenic Artists. New York also contains a handful of smaller, non-union shops which build some off-Broadway, industrial and small touring shows. On occasion a small non-union shop can act as a subcontractor for specialty work on a Broadway show.

Likewise, lighting equipment must be rented from a lighting rental shop under IATSE jurisdiction; smaller shops exist for rental to off-Broadway and some touring companies. Costumes, too, for Broadway, must come from union shops. Here, the stitchers are Theatrical Costume Workers, a branch of the International Ladies Garment Workers Union. And here too, special projects may be sub-contracted to a small non-union shop or group of craftspeople.

We will explain more about the workings of the unions, and their membership requirements in a later chapter. What this means to us now that we are in the process of getting a show assembled is that there are only four or five of each kind of shop (scenery, lights, costumes, sound) available to us to choose from in the area.

The process of choosing a shop is basically the same for each department. Most often the decision is made by competitive bidding. For scenery and costumes, the Designers submit working drawings or costume plates to the shop. Our Producer will purchase the sets and costumes, so the price that it bids will include the cost of materials and labor, and will be sufficient to cover the shop's overhead. Lighting and Sound Designers submit a list of the equipment which they require. Most lighting and sound gear is rented. The Producer will pay a down payment, a percentage of the value of the equipment which covers the first weeks of the rental period. After that, a smaller fee, often a fraction of a percent of the equipment's value, is charged for each week that the equipment is used. At the conclusion of the run of the show, the equipment is returned to the shop. The Producer's final bill is for any equipment that may be broken or missing.

From the drawings or lists submitted, the manager of each shop or studio submits a price to the Producer, or more likely to his General Manager. Negotiations are carried on, and contracts are signed with one or more of each kind of shop. Musicals with very elaborate scenery may come to an agreement whereby the work is shared by several shops—scenery for the 1982 production of *Cats* was built by three scenic studios; large props which created the show's atmosphere of an oversized garbage dump were contributed by an additional five shops or studios. Yet another firm was responsible for animation, mechanics and hydraulics. The lighting equipment came from a single rental house, but another firm, whose specialty is special effects, supplied a large and complicated neon sign.

The process of bids and bargaining has taken place with our show. The contracts are signed. In separate parts of New York City, people are beginning to work on the scenery, lighting, costumes, sound and properties. Let's visit them and discover who they are and what they are up to.

THE LIGHTING RENTAL SHOP

It comes as a surprise to some people to realize that all of the lighting equipment for a Broadway show is either rented or purchased by the Producer of that show. Remember, when we were backstage on opening night and mentioned that only two weeks before, the theatre had been empty? Empty means a bare box with four walls, a pipe grid, and electrical service. All of the lighting instruments, the console from which they are controlled, the pipes and stands from which they are suspended, and the cable with which they are connected, are rented. The light bulbs (which Electricians refer to as *lamps*), the tinted plastic sheets which go in front of the lighting units and impart color to the beams of light (*color* or *gel,* from an earlier time when, instead of plastic, thin sheets of colored gelatin were used), along with such items as spare fuses for the control system are referred to as *perishables,* and are purchased from the lighting rental house.

The other part of the lighting plot that will have to be purchased will be any complicated special lighting effects made specifically for this production. Our show has several very long strings of tiny twinkling lights which hang from a pipe behind a *translucent* (light can be seen through it) drop in the summer night scene. They will be purchased. The huge bunches of flowers that drop in from the flies after the brass pot has turned into a bunch of roses, also light up. As soon as the prop maker has built the flowers, they will be shipped to the electric shop to be wired. This, too, will be purchased, not rented.

There are two classifications of Electricians working in the shop. The employees of the shop are responsible for locating the necessary equipment in the storage areas, making sure that it is in good condition, both electrically and mechanically, and ready for the show electrician. The employees of the show, a Production Electrician and one or two Assistant Electricians, spend usually two weeks in the shop, organizing their particular production. They must be signed to a union contract before they can begin this work, and must show the contract to the Union Shop Steward before they can start.

The *Shop Foreman* supervises all of the work that goes on in the shop. He supplies the shop electricians with lists of equipment that must be readied for each of the several shows that may be in production at the same time. He answers questions of both the shop and show Electricians, finds things that the show Electricians need, and orders necessary supplies and new equipment. He is often on the telephone, talking with Electricians who are out of town on a tryout tour or a road tour and need supplies or additional equipment. He's very patient, very busy, and never seems to stop moving.

Although most of the Shop Electricians can do any of the work demanded in the shop, since it is organized into areas, they tend to have specialties.

In one end of a space a city block long, and nearly as wide, one or two people are checking out lighting control systems. Their meters and other test gear are rather sophisticated, and some of their tools seem quite delicate. Most of the lighting control on Broadway is done with computerized control systems. Although the first such lighting control system on Broadway appeared in 1975, with the opening of *A Chorus Line,* the revolution from cumbersome, manually operated "piano boards" (named for their size) took place within five years. Small shows may have their lighting controlled by pre-set boards the size of an attache case, connected to a small suitcase-sized group of dimmers. (The levers or handles which are manipulated in order to change the lights are called *faders* or *controllers*; the container of electronic gear that actually makes the lights more or less bright is called a *dimmer*.) Still in use to some degree are larger lighting control panels, consisting of 6, 8, 12, or 24 autotransformer dimmers, whose control is electric rather than electronic.

One of the larger areas of the shop consists of shelves filled with "spotlights." They are referred to by the Electricians as *Lekos* (the long, tubular lights), and *Fresnels* (the smaller, more nearly square ones with pressed concentric circles in their glass lenses). Both come in an assortment of sizes, the 3", 6" and 8" being most popular for theatrical use. Lekos give a sharper beam of light, which can be adapted, by changing their front barrels and glass lenses to cast a wider or narrower beam for distances from 10 to 100 feet. The smallest Broadway show uses over 100 of these lights; a large musical may have as many as 700.

Near the shelves of lekos and fresnels, a number of electricians are working at benches. Each has a list of the lights needed for one of the shows that is being put together in the shop. They select the proper kind and size of unit, make sure that it has the appropriate lens in good condition and a working lamp. They make sure that its screws are in tightly, its electrical connections secure, its wires unfrayed. They adjust the focus of the beam of light, make sure that the plug on the end of its short asbestos cords will make a good contact. The correct hanging hardware, a C-Clamp or sidearm, is attached. Finally, they will make sure that any exposed metal is covered with a coat of a dull, black, heat-resisting paint. Then the unit is added to a pile of lights ready for the show electrician.

Other shelves have other stage lighting units, used more infrequently than these warhorses. Other Electricians are similarly involved in a very thorough electrical and mechanical check of scoops, beam projectors, the six foot to twelve foot lengths of striplights which are used to light backdrops and sky cycloramas, and the large Xenon or carbon arc followspots, like the ones that were playing around the empty house as we walked in on opening night. When the show starts to set up in the theatre, an additional show Electrician, the *Front Light Operator,* will be signed to a contract.

In still another part of the shop, we find a large, electrically operated drum, about three feet in diameter. For every lighting unit in the show, there is a piece of heavy stage cable, from 25 to 200 feet in length. Each piece of cable is tested electrically. Frays are taped, damaged connectors are replaced, one connector is inserted into a slot in the drum, and the drum turns and winds the cable into a more manageable coil.

Other supplies which may be needed, iron boom stands and bases, long lengths of pipe, hanging hardware and the heavy asbestos cloths that hang behind light pipes for fire protection, lie on shelves, waiting to be assigned to a show.

As these materials are made ready for them, the Show Electricians label and pack them in boxes with careful lists and records. Lighting Designer Beverly Emmons once began a lecture by saying that lighting was about numbers. The Show Electricians are demonstrating this right now. It is most important that the hundreds of pieces of equipment and cable for a show be organized so that they can be unloaded and mounted in the theatre as quickly and efficiently as possible. On the Lighting Designer's plot, each horizontal pipe has a number, and each light hanging from that pipe is numbered sequentially. Each vertical pipe, or boom is also numbered, and lettered L or R for the side of the stage on which it is located. Each lighting unit on the boom is also numbered sequentially. The Show Electricians are painting these numbers, in white paint, on each Leko and Fresnel. "#2 - 17" means that this unit is the seventeenth light hanging from the number two electric pipe. When all of the lights for a particular location are assembled and marked, they are packed together in a box. Three copies of a listing of the contents of the box are made. One copy is taped or stapled to the inside of the box lid, one remains at the shop, one stays in the Electrician's files. Accessories, such as hardware and asbestos cloth are packed in the appropriate box.

The same procedure goes for the cable. The female connector is marked with the pipe and instrument number for which it is designated; the male end is marked with the number of the controller to which that light will be assigned. Most often, for efficiency of the load-in, cables are taped together in bundles of from six to ten. The bundle is labeled with a tag, saying perhaps "#2 - 6-100'/150'," meaning that these six cables bundled together are from one hundred to one hundred fifty feet long, and belong to the second electric pipe.

Naturally, all of the cables for a single pipe are packed together in a box, and three copies of the box list are made. Most often, the Electrician will allow several extra, unassigned cables on each pipe, in case one fails, or so that, should one of the many changes that may be made in rehearsals and early previews involve adding a light, there will be a cable nearby to connect to it. These cables are marked too, with an "X" for extra. And there is even an "extras" box, with spare units, spare cables, and three copies of its list.

The Show Electrician may also be running around town shopping. There are "practicals" in our show, lighting fixtures, things like wall sconces, hanging lamps and table lamps. These are chosen by the Scenic Designer, although the Electrician is likely to have the addresses of some special sources for such things in his files. The Electrician is responsible for procuring them, making any necessary adaptations in their wiring, and packing them. Yes, they go on a list, too. With the people from the shop who are working on the *specials* (those twinkling star garlands and the light-up roses that the show is buying), he checks those out, makes sure that he understands their workings, and that his Electrician's workbox contains any replacement parts that he may need for them.

The Electrician's workbox is checked for supplies. The workbox is about the size of a steamer trunk, and is stocked with perishables— spare lamps, gel, marking tape, glow tape, heavy cloth ("gaffer") tape, a wide variety of hand and small power tools, and a myriad of screws, washers, nuts and bolts and "good junk" such as might be found in a busy tinkerer's basement. Like the Stage Manager, the Production Electrician prides himself in being prepared for most emergencies that may arise.

And finally, the Electrician or his assistant is preparing the color for the show. The thin sheets of plastic are cut to the size of a frame which fits in slots at the front of the unit. The color's identifying number is marked on each sheet with a grease pencil, the sheet is inserted in the frame which is labeled with the pipe and instrument number. The prepared gel frames are organized by pipe and packed together. A spare set of gel frames is taken along, to make color changes easier.

All of the boxes are packed and the box lists made. The boxes are not cardboard cartons, but sturdy wooden travelling cases, with castered bottoms, for ease in moving. Each box is labeled with the show name and a number. The iron pipe and bases are gathered together and labeled. A master list of boxes is made. A truck or trucks of the proper size is arranged for. The lights are ready to go.

THE SOUND RENTAL SHOP

There are many similarities between a sound rental shop and a lighting rental shop. In both places, there are quantities of equipment stored in an organized fashion; in both places this equipment is tested and overhauled by Shop Technicians; in both places this equipment is labeled and organized by show technicians, in this case the Sound Operators. The differences lie in the specific nature of the work and the type of equipment.

Sound equipment includes *sources which generate sound signals* (microphones, tape decks and pick-ups for electronic instruments); *amplifiers* which expand the sound signals; and a *console* at which the Sound Operator controls the shaping, mixing and equalizing of the sound signal, and at which he may further alter it by adding echo or reverberation effects. Finally, at the control console, the Sound Operator will assign the controlled sound signal to the last component of the system, the *speakers.*

There is a great deal of both microphone and speaker cable on any show. With the exception of the wireless microphones, all elements of the sound system, including the output element of the wireless microphone receivers, must be connected to the control console.

The Shop Technicians check the equipment carefully, with meters and oscilloscopes.

The Sound Operators make sure that the microphones and speakers have labels, indicating where, on stage or in the house, they will be located. Each piece of equipment is assigned a number. Most important are the labels on both ends of each of the many lengths of cable. Each cable is assigned a number which is labeled on both cable ends. Detailed "track sheet" records are kept of the number assignments of the equipment and of the cable to which each piece is attached. As with the detailed labeling of lighting equipment, this will allow the set-up of the equipment to proceed efficiently and more quickly.

The equipment is organized and packed in road boxes. There is a microphone box and several boxes of cables, with box lists and labels. The console, speakers, and racks into which the tape decks have been mounted are likely to have custom built cases, crafted to fit them exactly. In the extras box are spare microphones and amplifiers and cables, a generous supply of each type of fuse needed for the equipment, and a collection of connectors and cable, should special cables have to be made up.

The Sound Operator's work box includes an array of small screw drivers, pliers and cutters, solder and a soldering iron, meters, and a supply of labels and markers. There is a tape splicer and leader tape. There are also operating manuals for each piece of equipment, with circuit diagrams, and a blueprint of the wiring and hook-up of the entire system.

In yet another box are packed both of the Stage Manager's Communication Systems, the intercom over which we will call the show and the intercom to the Dressing Rooms, with emergency standby systems for each. Control boxes, power supplies, headsets, remote stations ("biscuits") and quantities of cable are included. So are spares of everything. Also in this box are the speakers which will carry the sound of the show to the dressing rooms, wardrobe room and other off-stage areas, the microphones, controller and connecting cables for this system.

During this pre-production time, the Sound Operator, as well as organizing and labeling the equipment and cables in the shop, may be working with the Sound Designer on the preparation of the sound effects tape. The sounds are collected from various sources—records, sound libraries, tapes which they record in a studio or "in the field," for this particular show. In a sound studio, these are assembled into a reel of "show tape" with the individual cues in order, separated by labeled leader tape. Two copies of the tape are made for the show. The Master Tape is held on file at the studio, should changes or further copies need to be made.

THE SCENE SHOP

Probably the first place we'd see in a tour of a scene shop would be the office. It is a rather small room, with drafting tables as well as desks, and book shelves filled with hardware and equipment catalogs. A large window usually looks out onto the working space. This is where records are kept and work is planned. The *Layout Man* is sitting at one of the drafting tables. He and the Shop Foreman are discussing the details of construction of one of the big wagon units on our set. Although the Scenic Designer has supplied the shop with "working drawings" which are to scale and indicate the construction of each piece, the shop may feel, with a particularly complex piece of construction, that it is necessary to do further work on paper before they begin building.

The Shop Foreman, with the shop manager, has spent a good deal of time with the Scenic Designer before they have come up with their price for building the show. They have discussed alternate and perhaps more inexpensive ways of achieving what the Scenic Designer wants. They have asked the Scenic Designer to specify all of the materials. If a vital piece of hardware cannot be obtained in time for it to be used on our set, they will suggest alternatives and help figure out a way for it to be done.

The traditional "basic building block" of a stage set is the *flat*. It is a rectangular frame, made of wood, usually 1″ x 3″ pine, with one or more horizontal pieces for reinforcement. A stage setting with one or two interior spaces will be made up of nothing but flats, some of which will have windows, doorways or archways in them. This kind of simple set would not require the shop to do any drafting to supplement the Scenic Designer's working drawings. Our set is a very skeletal abstract shape, constructed from metal and several kinds of plastic as well as wood. As the show progresses through the characters' lives, other bits of scenery attach to this shape, or unfold from it. Since we won't have time to figure out how all this goes together after we load the set into the theatre, it must be thought out very thoroughly now, on paper. The Shop Foreman and the Layout Man are working out the details of the construction and hardware needed to effect the scenery changes now.

Let's walk around the shop and see what is here before the work day really starts, when the noise of the power tools and the activity makes it hard to find out what's going on. Not far from the big rolling loading doors are the lumber racks, which are storage docks against one wall into which raw materials are unloaded from the lumber yard and the metal suppliers. There is a truck pulled up to the door, and lengths of 1 x 3 and 2 x 4, and dozens of 4' x 8' sheets of plywood are being put into the labeled places in the lumber rack. The truck is delivering the lumber for our set, since the Shop Foreman has already studied the Scenic Designer's working drawings with great care, and made a thorough list of all of the supplies that will be needed to build it. Lumber, metals, hardware and plastics will be delivered in the next few days. Since each set is different, and since the materials needed for construction take up a great deal of space, the shop keeps very few materials on hand. They are ordered for each show.

Beyond the lumber rack is a large table. Beside it is a pull-over saw. A table saw and a band saw are nearby. This is the cutting, marking and assembly area.

A large table beyond is where the flats or other pieces of scenery will be covered with canvas or plywood. Nearby is a steel shelving unit filled with a great many precisely labeled bins. This is where the hardware is kept. There is a drill press and a sander nearby.

Off in another well-ventilated corner is the metal-working area. Here, we find another drill press, a power hacksaw or perhaps a horizontal bandsaw. There is also an arc welder, a portable oxy-acetylene welder and a MIG welder, and a bench grinding wheel.

A tool area under one of the work tables contains a router, skill saws, sabre saws, finish sanders and power drills.

Next to a window is a clear area with a work table. This is where work is done with plastics.

One way of describing the job of the Shop Carpenter is that it involves the skilled operation of all of the tools mentioned above. Yes, hand tools, hammers and saws and wrenches and squares and levels and planes are used too. The individual worker brings these with him. Before we go on to look at the paint area, the other large part of the shop, let's track a piece of scenery through the tour we've just taken, and see how it gets built.

The building process is, of course, not unlike the process you go through when building a bookcase in your basement, although, since this is a much bigger project, the steps are perhaps more precise and organized. The Shop Foreman first divides the work up into logical units. The six pieces of wall for our living room are a unit; the three doorways are a unit. The abstract framework that is the basic part of our set seems to divide itself into three units. With the drawings for each unit, those from the Scenic Designer and the detailed drawings that the Layout Man has done, goes a work order, listing the various steps in building, in the order in which they must be done. First there is a *cutting list*. Each of the six living room flats is to be 12 feet tall and 3 feet wide. The 1 x 3 lumber that arrived today is 2 ⅝" wide. Each flat will have two horizontal supports. The cutting list for 1 x 3 will indicate twelve 3' pieces (tops and bottoms of the frames), twelve pieces 11' 6 ¾" (the sides), and twelve pieces 2' 6 ¾" (the horizontal supports), and six 2' 6" cross braces, each of their ends cut to a 45° angle.

Any necessary details about construction are noted on the work order. Four of these flats will be covered with canvas; the two on the end will be covered on both sides with plywood, so that they can be wood panelled walls in the living room, and then swing in for the dance hall, revealing the art deco murals and grey silk draperies for that set. The differences in construction technique for these two are indicated; there is a cutting list for the plywood covers, and the exact position at which the mirrors attach is shown. The placement for the hinges on the two end panels is indicated. The work order goes to the shop floor.

First, all of the cutting and marking is done on a particular unit. Each measurement is made twice, and the length is checked after it is cut. The length of each piece and the number or code of that unit (upstage wall #1, for example) is written on it. Then the unit is put together on the assembly table, most often with plywood triangles ("corner blocks") and rectangles ("keystones") secured with nails or staples shot from a pneumatic gun. A great deal of care is taken. There will not be time to correct careless mistakes in the theatre.

The next step is gluing and stapling the covering (canvas or plywood) onto the frames. Any hardware that is necessary to attach them one to another is put on. So are the hinges which permit the end units to turn in. The fabric covered flats are given a "size coat" of paint, white, with a slight tint of color to make it easier to see if it is even. The paint shrinks the fabric slightly, making the covering taut.

Then it is time for the trial set-up. Space is cleared; the flats are put together as they will be in the theatre. The Carpenters and Shop Foremen check their work. Does it look, structurally, like the plan? Does it fit together properly? Perhaps some adjustments will have to be made. A long length of wood, a *batten,* is cut to run across the four flats that do not move, to stabilize them. It is temporarily attached and it is marked "upstage wall, center batten." It will go to the theatre with the rest of the set, ready to be installed. The Scenic Designer is around for the trial set-up; one Stage Manager is too, particularly concerned with any complicated piece of scenery that actors may have to climb on, jump on, slam, or perform any complicated movements against. We've been at rehearsals, and we know exactly how the set will be used. We make a note for the costumer that a doorway looks narrow for the actress' entrance in a long full skirt. We suggest that a door may need additional bracing, because it now gets slammed very violently in a quarrel scene. Adjustments are made, and the scenic unit moves to another part of the shop, the paint area.

Painting is done in another room, or on another floor of the building. There is sawdust in the air in the carpentry area, and this would interfere with painting. The paint area is basically a lot of clear space. There must be room on the floor to lay a *drop,* a piece of fabric the size of the full stage (perhaps fifty feet wide and twenty feet high). Painting is most often done with the scenic unit lying flat on the floor. The painters use brushes with long extension handles. In the paint area, there is, of course, a deep slop sink; a source of water to mix paint, and a place to wash brushes. The brushes are for the most part fine hog bristle, in a variety of sizes from ¼ inch to six inches. Like the carpenter's hand tools, the individual painters come to work bringing their own brushes. Water base paints are used for most scenery, although special, heavy-duty enamels may be used on floors and special pieces.

Above, craftperson Robin Cocking is working on a piece of decorative moulding at Hudson Scenic Studios. Below, carpenter Michael Sabella is attaching a leg to a full-stage platform for the Broadway production of *Moose Murders*. Twelve carpenters worked for three weeks to complete the set in the shop; the show closed after one performance. Photos: R. Harden.

Several layers of paint are likely to be applied to each piece of scenery. Even a wall that is seemingly one color is likely to have a fine spray in another shade, to add depth and to help indicate light and shadow. The spray is applied with a compression tank to which is attached a wand-type spray head, rather like a garden fogger.

Remember the painter's elevations which were the last thing that the Scenic Designer prepared? Here they are in the paint shop, carefully protected by a sheet of plastic. The painters must, in large scale, exactly duplicate the color swatches and the design that the designer has indicated. In a union situation, designers cannot paint their own scenery; they must be very clear in their instructions.

There is a hot plate in the paint area, too. Yes, of course there's a coffee pot on it, but it is also used to heat water for mixing dyes. Painting with dyes, so that light can glow through from behind a drop or set piece, is often done. The colors of dyes are much more brilliant than the colors of pigments, hence some fine detail may be painted with dye.

In the construction area, beyond the Shop Foreman and the Layout Man (who may, in a smaller shop, be one and the same), everybody pretty much does everything. Most often the same group of from two to ten workers will carry the building of a unit to completion, doing the measuring, cutting, assembly and finish work. In the paint shop, jobs become a bit more specific. The *Charge Painter* is the paint shop equivalent to the Shop Foreman. The Charge Painter supervises the work and is the liaison between the Scenic Designer and the crew. The Charge Painter can do any type of painting. The *Layout People* plan the work. For a drop, or a unit with a great deal of detail, chalk lines are snapped to make a grid. With a similar but smaller grid, to scale on the painter's elevation, an ornate pattern or picture can readily be sketched in with charcoal. Some patterns are drawn on large sheets of brown paper; the outline is marked with a toothed wheel, similar to a pattern marker for fabric. The paper pattern is then taped to the drop or scenic unit, and a small muslin bag of powdered charcoal is pounded along the lines of the perforations. When the paper is removed, an indication of the line remains on the scenery. This is the work of the Layout Person, and is called *cartooning.*

The large areas of paint, which are first applied, are painted by *Lay-In Painters.* The final coats of most skilled brushwork are done by *Detail Painters. Shopmen* care for the equipment, do routine paint mixing and clean brushes and buckets.

Painters frequently find themselves working with materials other than paints and dyes. Real wall paper may be used, wood panelling may need to be stained and varnished, texture may be added to a piece of scenery by coating it with spackle. Sawdust or sand may be added to the base coat for texture.

Obviously the carpentry Shop Foreman and the Charge Painter work together in organizing the work, so that there is a smooth flow through the different areas, planning the process so that the painters will be working on a complicated drop that may take several days to complete while the Carpenters are building the most time-consuming units. The back side of all the scenic units is painted for fireproofing, and the union "bug," a symbol with the union shop number of this particular shop, is stencilled on the back of each piece. As each unit is completed, it is stored compactly, awaiting load out to the theatre.

THE COSTUME SHOP

Before the costume shop is decided upon, the Costume Designer has met with the managers of several of the shops in the city. They review sketches, discuss types of materials with the Designer, and solicit whatever information they need to know in order to determine a price for the costumes. How must each garment be constructed? Will the actor have to change from this to the next costume in a matter of seconds? If so, the costume must be made in such a way that the change is easily done. How many costumes are there? What kinds of fabric are being considered? Is there any painstaking handwork, such as beading or embroidery involved? Will craftspeople be needed to paint or dye? Eventually, the Producer is given a price by the shop, often broken down to price per costume. Both the Costume Designer and the shop know at this point that there are likely to be changes, additions and deletions as fabrics and finishing is decided upon, and the bid will likely spell out terms to be applied to these. The producer, in consultation with the Costume Designer, determines what shop or shops will be responsible for constructing the costumes. For a very expansive show, two or more shops may be involved, one doing principal costumes and one chorus, or one doing men and one women. One shop may do only the dance costumes. Specialized crafts work, beading, painting, soft sculpture, leather work, macrame, embroidery and the like may be done in the shop, or may be sub-contracted to one of the smaller shops that specialize in this work.

Our show has only two characters, but it covers over 50 years in time. Each actor, as it is now planned, will have twelve costumes. A shop is chosen and work begins. What kinds of jobs are available in a costume shop?

The Shop Foreman of a costume shop is the overall supervisor. He or she is responsible for assigning other workers to their tasks, for trouble-shooting, solving problems and answering questions, much like the Foreman of the lighting rental shop. The Shop Foreman keeps very close track of the progress of a show, for there is a deadline by which time the costumes must be delivered. The Shop Foreman may do some cutting or other work on a costume, because it is very likely that he or she has, at one time or another, done most of the jobs in the shop.

First, fabrics must be found and decided upon. This is the work of the *Shoppers*. Through consultation with the Costume Designer and the Shop Foreman, the Shopper discovers what kind of fabrics are needed for a particular group of costumes and sets out to find them. First, he or she needs information about the Designer's choice of color range and weight of fabric; should it be a fluttery sheer, or a heavy brocade? Is it important to the Costume Designer that it be a natural fiber—linen, cotton, silk or wool—or will a synthetic be acceptable? Obviously, they need some rough indication of the amount of fabric to be used; things available in one and two yard lengths as remnants may be fine for trim, but less satisfactory for a sweeping cape. How must the costume move? What kind of a drape should the fabric have? What kind of "hand"—how should it feel? The Costume Designer has been looking at fabrics, and the studio contains a number of samples and swatches, so that a request can be made for "something that moves like *this*, but in an earth color and more saturated," or "*this*, but real silk, with a smaller print."

Armed with this information, the Shopper hits the streets of the city. Since New York is the center of the nation's garment industry, there are many places to choose from: shops in the Designer's building, to which only fashion and design professionals can gain admittance; huge wholesale fabric warehouses; small specialty shops dealing in fine imported silks; a store on a side street with a reputation for carrying a vast array of "glitz", showy, metallic-threaded theatrical fabrics.

Trims must also be searched out. There are firms in the city that specialize in beads, in feathers, in artificial flowers, in sequins and decorative tapes. The Shopper discovers what might possibly fill the Designer's requests and holds to the Shop Foreman's budget. Samples are brought back, with a great deal of information about each sample. Where was it found? What does it cost? If a large quantity is needed, what is the price break if an entire bolt (usually about 60 yards) is purchased? Does the shop have a lot of it, or is it in limited supply? Can more be ordered from the mill? If so, can it be ordered and received in time for the costumes to be ready to load out of the door some four weeks hence? What other colors does it come in?

The Costume Designer, with the Shopper and the Shop Foreman, reviews these samples that have been brought back, handling them, playing with them, overlaying them one against the other, looking at them in combinations that may be on stage together, and gradually, decisions are made.

Certainly this is not a simple process. It may take the Shopper weeks to find a specific material, or to find, absolutely, that it doesn't exist. Something that a Shopper picks up, almost on whim, may change the Designer's idea about a costume, and, although very different from the first idea, fill the bill. Or it may suggest something yet again, and the Shopper is again off searching.

And this process varies from show to show. In a play about Army life, the shopper is looking for fabrics in a rather limited color range. In the musical *Nine,* with a cast of one man and twenty-two women, the Shoppers spent their time seeking out elegant and fragile silks, nets and imported brocades.

Sometimes a Costume Designer will have a very specific picture in their head, "pin-striped burgundy wool," "changeable silk in black and green," "blue denim." Compromises are made. A plain fabric will be beaded if exactly the right "glitz" cannot be found, stripes will be painted on, a lighter fabric will be backed, or cut differently.

It is not, however, just to fabric and trimming stores that the shoppers go. Stage costumes are sometimes made of the most unexpected materials! We know a Designer who within one year, draped his actors quite well in window screen mesh, movie projection screen, frosted plastic, pressed vinyl tablecloth material, and the silver diffraction grating with which car addicts adorn automobile bumpers. Shoppers often feel that they are on an 8-hour a day scavenger hunt.

Sometimes a decision is made to "make up" a fabric. Strips of ribbon may be sewn as stripes on a fabric, overlayed with tapes or lace and sequins. And the Shopper is off to locate what is needed.

Naturally, everything that they are looking for is not a challenge. The shop has regular sources of things that they use all the time—"pearl" beads, metal uniform buttons, basic colors of ribbons in all widths, things like black velvet and red velour. Bolts of taffeta and muslin, used for linings, are already on hand. Within a day, much that is needed can be ordered.

The costumes evolve. Some take longer than others. Changes and compromises are reached. Decisions are made.

The *Cutters* are the next important people to be galvanized into action. A single cutter will be responsible for overseeing the completion of a group of garments, from start to finish. From the Designer's sketch, the Cutter determines how the garment will be patterned, and how much fabric will be needed. The fabric is purchased and delivered.

By this time, back at the rehearsal hall, the play has been cast, and one of the first things that the Stage Managers have done is arrange for measurements to be taken of the actors and the stand-bys, who will have their own set of costumes made. The measurement form is long and detailed: wrist, head, glove size, shoulder to wrist, in addition to the basic chest, waist, hips and height. From the measurement chart and the costume sketch, the Cutter figures out, with advice and consent from the Costume Designer, how the garment will be constructed, and drafts any necessary patterns. The shop has a range of stock patterns for costume parts—simple blousey sleeves, knee britches, collars of various shapes, but many must be figured out for this show, with the help of geometry, a dressmaker's curve, a ruler and a T-square. A single sleeve, its middle pointed like an artichoke, or with ballooning insets, may have as many as 32 pattern pieces.

A *First Hand* works with each cutter as the patterns are made, laid out on the fabric in the most economical way, and cut. Together they have planned all of the steps that will be involved in the garment's construction.

It is time for the *Stitchers* to go to work. And that is what they do—stitch. They are skilled at operating sewing machines: very rapidly on simple seams, carefully on intricate ones, always with precision. A single stitcher will usually do all of the basic sewing on an individual garment. This is custom work, not a factory assembly line. Their work is sturdy and will hold up. Stage costumes get as much hard wear as the play overalls of an active four year old. They are made to last. And remember, these stitchers may be working with materials like the plastic window screens or slippery plastics that were mentioned above.

The last people to be involved, in many costumes, are the *Finishers*. Finishing may involve handwork, the application of patterns and trim. Some delicate fabrics must be hand hemmed. Still, the Cutter, with his or her First Hand, are supervising the costume that they patterned from the Designer's sketch.

It is also likely that a number of specialty workers will be involved in the construction and finishing of some costumes. A *Tailor* will be responsible for a great deal of the padding and construction of men's suits and overcoats. Other specialists who may be in the shop include *Dyers, Beaders, Painters, Millinery Specialists, Mask Makers, Armour Makers and Leatherworkers.*

Dyers obviously dye fabrics and costumes, sometimes in one color, as you might dye a shirt, using fabric dye from the dime store. But more often Dyers apply ombré patterns, changing hue or tint, top-dying, giving a random, textured effect to the fabric or using hot wax to make a batik effect. They know how much of what kind of dye to use to match the color on a Designer's sketch. They know how each type of synthetic or natural fabric will react to the various types of dyes. They work in a well-ventilated space, wearing rubber gloves, and for some powdered dyes, face masks, since the particles of dye may be injurious to lungs.

Beaders apply beads to make patterns and designs. It is painstaking handwork, and requires training to do efficiently and well.

Painters paint patterns on costumes. Using special paints that tend not to stiffen fabric, they may paint freehand with a brush, use a stencil with a brush or sponge, or create delicate shaded effects with an airbrush.

Millinery Specialists make hats. Starting with a heavy, stiff buckram frame, they cover it with fabric and add trims of ribbons, feathers, flowers or lace. Hand work is done with a needle or a hot glue gun.

Masks, Armour and Leatherwork may be done by a specialist in the shop, or sent out for a craftsperson to work on in his or her own studio. Masks can be fabric-based, moulded from a sheet polymer which becomes flexible with the application of a solvent ("Celastic"). Masks are also sculpted by applying heat to acrylic plastics, sculpted with scissors from blocks of urethene foam, formed by shaping pieces of light metal tubing or of wicker, moulded from liquid rubber in a plaster mask of the actor's face, or carved from light balsa wood. The Designer has determined, after discussions with the Director and the Choreographer, how the masks are to be used by the performers and what their basic look should be, but frequently consults with the mask maker about what types of materials will be used.

Armour can be stitched, glued, welded or moulded, using some of the mask techniques, and has been made from vacu-formed plastic, vinyl, rubber, automobile tires, Celastic, leather or metal. Suits of chain mail are sometimes crocheted or knitted from packing twine and painted to resemble metal.

Some leatherwork is done in the costume shop. Shoes can be custom made by one of the several large dance shoe companies in the city, or by a leatherworker in his or her studio. As with the mask and armour makers, the Costume Designer consults with these artisans about materials and methods.

Each garment requires at least two fittings, sometimes more. Most often, the actor will come to the costume shop for fittings. The fittings are done by the Designer and the Cutter. Finishers may be consulted about final details.

Costume workers soon learn to be gentle, delicate and considerate with actors at fittings. Actors are much more affected by the clothes they wear on stage than by the scenery they walk around in, the props they handle or the lights that illuminate them. They are aware of their bodies' real or imagined flaws. They have, like most of us, strong preferences about the color and cut of what they wear. And they are, in the process of rehearsals, building the characters who would and will wear these costumes. They may find the costume ill-fitting to the nature of the person they are constructing inside of it. They must be listened to, treated always with consideration and tact. Differences are discussed, compromises are reached, decisions are made.

And meanwhile, changes are being made back at the rehearsal hall. Perhaps the oldest tenet of playwriting is that "plays are not written, but re-written." The re-writing process starts early in rehearsals, and we are all aware that it may cease only with opening night. Re-writes may involve changes in costume, sets and lights, additions and subtractions. A ball-gown finished yesterday may be written out today, and a different one added tomorrow. The Designers and shop workers know that changes may come, and they adjust to them. The creative process is often not orderly. The atmosphere may at times become a bit hectic, but these people are geared to the unexpected, roll with the punches and continue their work. In a matter of weeks, the costumes are completed.

STAGE PROPERTIES

Any item in the world can be a stage property, from a paper clip to a fantastic ten foot high plant that seems to eat people. Acquiring a prop can be as easy as a trip to the dime store. It can also be a complex process involving days of telephone inquiries, detailed discussions, pages of engineering drawings and a good deal of trial and error.

Stage properties are collected by the *Property Master or Mistress.* It is the *Scenic Designer's* responsibility to specify and approve of the props' appearance; it is the Stage Manager's responsibility to communicate information about the way in which they are used which might affect their design or construction. A table that must be danced upon will be built differently from a table whose only function is to hold a telephone. A tray that must be carried through a doorway should not be wider than that doorway. If books simply sit on a shelf, they can be "faked" by gluing a row of book spines together. If actors must take the books from the shelves and open them, they must be "practical"—real books.

On Broadway, stage properties are either merchandised, rented, purchased or built.

Properties that are merchandised are given to the production, usually by the manufacturer, in exchange for the advertising value of a "credit" line in the program acknowledging the source. Beverage containers, packaged food products, luggage, stationery supplies, wrist watches, television sets and kitchen equipment and appliances are some of the articles that may be acquired in this way. New York has several Merchandizing Consultant Firms which make the necessary arrangements with manufacturers willing to provide such props.

Furniture, particularly antiques, art objects, weapons and office equipment are examples of articles that are often rented from shops, dealers or galleries. Arrangements for such rentals may be made by the Properties Person or the Scenic Designer or assistant.

If they cannot be merchandized, small items, such as paper goods, artificial flowers, dishes, linens and small bric-a-brac are purchased by the Scenic Designer's assistant or by the Properties Person, instructed by the Scenic Designer. Second hand stores are a popular prop supply source for many shows.

If a satisfactory prop cannot be found on the open market, the prop is built, sometimes by the scenic shop, sometimes by a specialized craftsperson skilled in welding, plastics work, machining, soft sculpture or whatever technique or techniques may be involved. The Scenic Designer is responsible for the look of the props, and specifies the construction method, frequently in consultation with the expert who will do the actual construction. The Scenic Designer provides working drawings for all shop-built props.

Scenic Designers and Properties Persons keep extensive files of stores in which almost any prop, from an abacus to a zebra skin, may be found. They also keep files on craftspeople who can construct any of the items that they might need.

SPECIAL EFFECTS

Another area of theatrical design and production, special effects, is sometimes a bit of a "catch-all" category, which may involve several departments. Special effects include devices which "make magic" on stage—scarves that turn into flowers, the harness and rigging upon which Peter Pan flies, a blob of ectoplasm which floats over the head of a medium, and the person-eating plant that we mentioned above. Unusual devices such as a car that belches smoke and moves on stage under its own power, a bottle that, without injury to an actor, can be broken over his head, a pistol that fires an umbrella are also special effects. So are atmospheric effects such as smoke, fog or falling snow. Purely mechanical effects (the scarf, ectoplasm, car, bottle, pistol and snow above) are the responsibility of the properties department. If the effect needs electrical power in order to work (the fog, perhaps the smoke and the plant; in our show, the roses that light up), the electrical department will be involved in its construction, and most often they will operate the effect during the show.

Some special effects, such as "break-away" bottles, are stock theatrical items that may be purchased from a theatrical supply house. Some, such as fog and bubble-making machines, are carried by lighting rental houses as stock items. Some are built by special craftsmen not connected with the theatre except for this job (the pistol that fires the umbrella would be built by a gunsmith). Some are built in one or more of the shops that build the show, from working drawings supplied by the Scenic and/or Lighting Designers or supplied by a Special Effects Consultant.

Consultants may be hired to work on a particular effect, or to do all of the effects on a show. Any show such as *Peter Pan* in which actors must fly will employ a Special Effects Specialist to design, build and supervise the operation of the apparatus. Many scene shops have staff with effects expertise; there are a few companies in the country, based near New York, Los Angeles or Las Vegas, which specialize in the design and building of special effects devices.

Everyone connected with the show has been kept busy. It is only days from "load in," the time that a completed set, costumes, props, lights, sound and special effects will appear at the theatre, be assembled, and our cast will be introduced to the physical elements of the production. Our prompt script is accurate, and there are blocking and technical notes on every page. If our work, and the work of the Designers and all of the people in the shops has been done well, we should have an easy time of it. We start concentrating more and more on how to get to opening night, putting all of the elements together so that the show can run.

Dress and technical rehearsals give the actors, director, and technical crews an opportunity to coordinate all the elements they have been preparing. Photo: NTC.

CHAPTER 5

GETTING IT TOGETHER

FINAL MEETINGS

As Stage Managers, we co-ordinate all of the theatrical "departments"—electrical, scenic, props, costumes, sound and special effects. Our particular area of concern is anything that affects the running of the show. We schedule a series of meetings with each department to insure that the show will run as smoothly as possible. In preparation, we have made sure that we have accurate notes on actors' blocking. With stop watches we have determined the duration of the sound cues, scene shifts and costume changes.

Costumes.   Our final meeting with the Costume Designer concerns costume changes. Although the most challenging fast changes for our stars are the twenty-second ones before the dance hall scene, there are a number of other changes taking from two to five minutes which will require the help of a dresser. There is not enough time for the actor to get to and from the dressing rooms, so the change will have to be done immediately in the off-stage area or "wings." Our blocking notes tell us which side of the stage the actors exit and enter. We have talked with the Scenic Designer to determine where the change areas can be set up, discovering that, for the scene shifts to move smoothly, the fast-change "booths" must be "struck" (removed) when not in use. Carpentry and Electrics have been told of the lights, folding screens, and tables they must supply; they have added the set-up and strike of these items to their list of duties.

At the final costume fittings, we rehearse the fast changes, the actor and dresser talking through what will happen. Their first "rehearsal" of the change takes 54 seconds; the second time it is down to 36 seconds; by the third time through, we realize that twenty seconds will not be a problem.

Properties and Special Effects.   We visit the electric shop, where the wiring of the special light-up roses is being completed. We operate the effect several times to be sure it works correctly.

We examine the properties that have been built and purchased. The way they look is the Scenic Designer's responsibility; we are concerned with the way they are used. A tray with bottles and glasses seems as though it might be too heavy for the leading lady to handle. Could the Property Mistress find some lighter weight items for the tray? The leading man has requested that, although he never opens it, there be some books and papers in his briefcase, so that it will not seem empty when he handles it. We pass this request on to the Property Mistress.

Scenery.   We meet with the Production Carpenter, the Flyman and the Scenic Designer, who has brought along the model of the set. We talk through what must happen in each set change and how much time is allowed. The Carpenter and Flyman begin to determine how many people will be needed for each shift, and exactly where each piece of scenery will be stored when it is not being used.

Lighting.   We go very carefully through the script with the Lighting Designer, discussing each lighting cue, and assigning each cue a number. Some of the cues, such as those at the beginning and ends of scenes, are already indicated in the script. Those which will show subtle changes of mood or emphasis will be requested by the Lighting Designer. The Lighting Designer has seen a run-through by this time. We try, from our blocking notes, to answer questions about where on stage the actors move during each scene. With this information, the Lighting Designer will make further decisions concerning which particular lights will be used in the scene. With her Assistant, the Lighting Designer sets about writing more numbers on paper. They prepare an *Instrument Schedule,* which summarizes the information on the Light Plot, instrument by instrument; a *Dimmer*

Schedule, listing what instruments are assigned to each controller, and a *"magic sheet,"* which, in graphic form, summarizes for the Lighting Designer which lights are focussed at which area of the stage. They also prepare a *Master Cue Tracking Form,* on which they can keep a running record of dimmer levels, from cue to cue. The "magic sheet" is for the reference of the Lighting Designer. The Assistant will consult the other forms during the lighting rehearsal, make changes, and record the Lighting Designer's work.

Sound. As with the Lighting Designer, we go through the script with the Sound Designer. We assign a cue number to each sound cue. Having timed the scenes during rehearsal, we can tell the Sound Designer how long each sound effect should last. We answer any further question the Sound Designer may have about the nature of the cue and the direction from which the sound should seem to be coming. The Sound Designer will also meet again with the Musical Director and the Composer. Together, they will make decisions affecting the placement of sound re-inforcement equipment for the instruments in the orchestra. Previously, with the Director, decisions have been made about sound re-enforcement for our stars.

FINAL RUN-THROUGH

Before we move the sets, lights, costumes and paraphernalia of the production into the theatre, we give the performers a chance to get used to the space by having a run-through of the entire show. The House Electrician has hooked up a couple of work lights; folding chairs indicate the placement of walls and furniture; the Musical Director will play the songs on the piano.

In the audience are friends of the cast and company, the Designers and their Assistants, and the Department Heads of the crews. The Sound Designer is taking careful notes and checking the running times of cues with a stopwatch. He also roams through the audience area, to try and get some sense of the way music and speech sound in that space. The Lighting Designer's eyes remain fixed on the stage, charting the movements of the actors. Occasionally she will whisper a terse note to her Assistant. Even though most of the costumes, sets and props are completed, the Scenic and Costume Designers watch the run-through carefully, perhaps visualizing their work on stage, certainly making note of anything they see that may involve changes in their designs.

The atmosphere after the run-through is friendly, but charged with the feeling of something about to happen. The actors, with the Director, have spent the last month rehearsing and refining what they will do on stage. In the next week and a half, the technicians, with the Designers, will do the same.

THE LOAD-IN

Work starts early the next morning. Large trucks arrive at the scenic shop, the lighting shop and the sound shop. The trucks are driven by members of the Theatrical Loaders and Haulers division of the Teamsters union. Each driver is assisted by a member of the same union, known as a *Loader.*

All of the material taken out of the electric shop, except for the pipes, is in castered road boxes. This is the first truck to be loaded and the first to arrive at the theatre. The sound equipment, also boxed, is loaded into its truck quickly. Loading the truck at the scenic shop is more complicated, since the sets are not boxed, and are of differing sizes and even ungainly shapes. It will take several truck trips to transport all of the scenery. The Master Carpenter has organized what will go into each truck. At the theatre he will start working upstage, while the Electricians will start downstage. Therefore, the first truck holds the basic skeletal structure, the walls that fly in front of it, other scenic units that play upstage, and the Carpenters' well-stocked work boxes.

Costumes will not be worn until the first dress rehearsal, a week away. It will be several days before the hampers and hangers of them arrive at the theatre, along with the iron, ironing board, sewing machine, notions and supplies that the Wardrobe Attendents will need to do their job.

The electrical equipment arrives at the theatre first; the boxes are unloaded into an interior alleyway. As they are needed, they are brought onstage and unloaded. Empty boxes will be collected the next day and trucked back to the shop. The Master Electrician, with his Assistant, has been at the shop, overseeing the loading of the truck. Once it is ready to leave, he hurries to the theatre. He meets the Chief Front Light Operator, who, like the Master Electrician and Assistant, is under contract for the show, and the 15 to 20 people who comprise the load-in crew. Some of these people may also have been hired to run the show. Some of them will only work the two or three days it takes us to install the show equipment in the theatre. Many of them are already working on their own shows in the evenings.

The second truck to arrive contains the sound equipment, which is unloaded into the auditorium area. The two Sound Operators, working with several of the Electricians from the load-in crew, begin to unpack and set up their equipment, first organizing the sound console in the audience area. The Electricians and the Carpenters will be very busy on stage. As they finish, the Sound Operators will have an opportunity to set up their speakers and run their cables.

The last truck to arrive is the first load of scenery. The Master Carpenter meets his crew of 15 to 20, and begins to install the set. Large pieces that are not yet needed on stage are laid over seats in the house. The Master Carpenter and Master Electrician break up their crews into smaller working groups, being careful not to get in each other's way.

The meticulous organization done in the shops is paying off in the efficiency of the set-up. A group of Carpenters is assembling the skeletal structure, using hardware from a bucket labelled "Up Center Unit #1." Other Carpenters are fastening the wall unit into place. Another group is hanging the *cyclorama,* the muslin and gauze "sky" curtain which is the farthest upstage scenic element.

Two electricians, working with the House Electrician, are connecting heavy electrical feeder cables to the theatre's main power supply. These cables will be connected to the dimmers, and the dimmers to the lighting control console. They will check to see that it is in working order. The Flyman lets in a set of lines; forty feet of pipe are attached to them. The lights that will hang from that pipe are lined up in order on the floor. Since each light is labeled with its pipe and instrument number, this is an easy task. Cable for that pipe, in the bundles that were made up in the shop, is stretched out on the floor. When the pipe is attached to the lines, they are secured, with the pipe about four feet off the floor, an easy working height for the lighting units to be attached. Each light is plugged into its proper cable (those, if you remember, were labeled in the shop also); the cable bundles are tied to the pipe, and it is flown to the proper height. The Flyman is a level above the stage on the *fly floor,* the walkway against one side of the wall from which the pipes are controlled. He raises or lowers pipes as requested by the Master Carpenter or Master Electrician. A shout of "Pipe coming in—HEADS" precedes each action, warning people out of the way.

By the end of the first day of the load-in, all of the equipment has arrived in the theatre. At noon on the second day, most of the large scenic pieces are assembled or hung. The Sound Operator has installed speakers in the house, and has hooked up the sound control console. All of the lights are hung, cabled and "plugged" (connected to their control circuit). The lighting control console is operational. It is time to focus the lights. This requires semi-darkness. The Carpenters, Sound Operators and Property People continue working as they can, in other areas than on stage if possible. The Electricians provide them with work lights as they can.

FOCUSING AND FINISHING

The Lighting Designer dictates the focus of each light. The Master Electrician climbs a sturdy A-frame ladder, which is held firmly by members of the crew. They will start working at one end of a pipe, and deal with each light, in order, across the pipe. A light is turned on from the control board. The Lighting Designer consults her light plot, which is spread out on a table near-by. She tells the Master Electrician where on stage the light should be directed. The instrument itself is then adjusted to make the beam of light softer or harder edged, larger or smaller, as the Designer wishes. On the elipsoidal reflector spotlights (Lekos), shutters which determine the shape of the beam of light are adjusted. Finally the color filter is inserted, and the designer moves on to the next light. Meanwhile, the Assistant Electrician waits on a ladder by the box boom lights. While one ladder is being moved, or while one Electrician is making a particularly intricate adjustment on a unit, the Lighting Designer will focus the lights hung in the other position. Occasionally the Lighting Designer will ask to look at a light already focussed in combination with one she is working on. An Electrician is standing by the control console, ready to bring lights on and off as requested. The Lighting Designer's Assistant is coping with paperwork, noting any changes of plugging, position or color on the records.

As they can, the Carpenters complete their set-up, the Sound Operators install and connect the on stage speakers and make their cable runs. Any cable that must lie on the floor is taped down securely. Carpet is laid over the cable and secured to the floor, so that no one will trip on the cable.

Starting times and lunch hours for the various crews are staggered, to give each crew some exclusive time on stage. At the end of the third day our show is basically installed in the theatre. There are still some details to be taken care of; the Scenic Designer and Properties Mistress have not finished "dressing the set" with pictures and bric-a-brac; perhaps there is still a curtain to be hung or a light to be moved. It is time to start technical rehearsals.

TECHNICAL REHEARSALS

First, it is the Carpenter's time. Each set is set up in turn. The exact method of changing the scenery from one set to the next has been worked out on paper by the Scenic Designer and the Master Carpenter. The moves are made, and changed if necessary. They determine what stagehand will do each scene shift, since, of course, the same stagehand will perform a particular move every night. The Stage Managers are watching and recording this process. There may be additional cues that we may have to call, telling a flyman when a particular pipe can come in, or giving a "GO" to a curtain puller who cannot see the stage. We must know the patterns of the shifts well enough to be able to keep the actors well out of the way of moving scenery. David and Ann are working at the theatre with the Designers and crew, and Richard is at the rehearsal hall with the actors.

The scenery work moves with dispatch. It is well planned, and we do not rehearse the shifts over and over. Proficiency will come with the technical run-throughs. Now we must begin lighting the show.

The Lighting Designer and her Assistant are sitting in the house, behind a table top about five feet long, spanning two rows of seats. The light plot is spread out on the table. Near the Assistant are those pieces of paper with numbers on them: the instrument schedule, dimmer schedule, and tracking sheet, which we mentioned earlier. Near the Lighting Designer is her "magic sheet" for quick reference. Both the Designer and Assistant are on headsets; there is a dim worklight on the table, and probably several containers of coffee.

The Electricians have checked the lights, bringing on each dimmer to see if the proper lights are connected to it, and are focussed in the proper place, gelled in the proper color. The scenery is set up for the first scene.

The Lighting Designer calls dimmer levels to the Master Electrician, who is on headset at the lighting control console. When the Lighting Designer wishes to see the lights on people, one Stage Manager will "stand in" for the actors. As the Lighting Designer is satisfied with the look of each cue, she will say "record that," and go on to the next cue. She gives each cue a *count,* the time which it should take to happen. Large scenic units and drops are placed in position as she needs them. She has an idea what lights she wishes to use in each scene. She may look at several combinations of lights before deciding the one she prefers. She works quickly. As they work through the show, she may ask her Assistant to make notes of changes to be made in color or focus—"work notes" to be done when the run through of cues is completed.

TECHNICAL RUN-THROUGHS

The next day we begin Technical Run-throughs. For the first time since the load-in, the actors are in the theatre, ready to work slowly and wait a lot. This is the Designers' and Technicians' time. The Director is seated next to the Lighting Designer at the production table. The Scenic Designer and Sound Designer are near by. The Designers are on headsets. The Sound Operators, Electricians, Carpenters, Flymen and Front Light Operators are all in position, where they will be on opening night. For this rehearsal, the Chief Front Light Operator is also on headset. The actors are not yet in costume, as the Costume Designer is likely attending to last minute details on them. Ann is at the Stage Manager's Desk on headset, in communication with the Lighting Designer and Sound Designer in the front of the house, as well as with the crew. Richard and David are also backstage. As we run through the show, they will make notes of any cues they must relay, and of the details they must check after each set-up. The rehearsal pianist begins to play the overture. Exact times are set for the house lights to go out, and for the house curtain to rise. The pianist cuts to the last 32 bars, and the show curtain flies out at the end of the overture, revealing the two stars seated by the hassock. The show curtain flies in and out several times, until the Director and Scenic Designer are satisfied that the correct speed has been found.

The Director suggests that the lights on the opening picture are not bright enough. The Lighting Designer explains that they will start to become brighter as the music box sound is heard, but asks the Electrician to raise dimmers 17, 18 and 19 one point. "Yes," says the Director, as the lights brighten a bit, "that's really better for an opening picture."

"Record that change," requests the Lighting Designer over the headset.

"Done. It's a part of the cue."

As the actress opens the music box, Ann calls the first sound cue.

"Too soft," says the Director. "Not enough presence."

The Sound Designer asks the Sound Operator to increase the volume. Neither Designer or Director are happy with the result. "Can I try just a little through the house speakers?" asks the Sound Operator over the headset.

"Good idea," says the Sound Designer. The Sound Operator adjusts the knobs on the console until the Director and Sound Designer are satisfied with the quality of the music box sound. Ann calls the next light cue, and more light comes up on the actors.

"Do you want lights with the sound cue, or just after?" asks Ann.

"Let's try it both ways," suggests the Director, and this is done. "At the same time as the cue, but not so fast!"

"Double the count, Board," says the Lighting Designer. "Take it in eight."

Very slowly, cue by cue, we proceed through the show. The actors take the time to adjust to the set and props that they will be using. The Scenic Designer makes notes of touch up painting that will have to be done. When the Director and Lighting Designer agree that the sunlight coming through a window should be brighter, the Scenic Designer offers to exchange the curtains for filmier ones. The Scenic Designer's Assistant makes a note to find the new curtains and arrange for them to be hung. The Lighting Designer continues to "paint with light," adjusting the levels of each scene. "There's too much spill on the upstage wall," she says to the Scenic Designer and the Director after one cue. "We'll have to wait until after the run to re-focus that light."

"Can the light be warmer here?" asks the Director, and once again the Lighting Designer calls for different dimmer levels, which are agreed on and recorded by both the Master Electrician and by the Lighting Designer's Assistant, on the tracking sheets.

"The crickets are distracting here," remarks the Director at one point. "Can we take them out just after the actors cross to down right, but bring them back after the song?" This adjustment is agreed to by the Sound Designer, and made by Ann in her Prompt Script and by the Sound Operators, who are writing the details of their cue sheets as the rehearsal progresses.

At another moment, the Lighting Designer asks, "Isn't it too bright all over right now? Shouldn't we maybe fade down slowly to light just on the area where the actors are?"

"Let's see it," says the Director.

"Light Board, let's see a thirty-count fade. All dimmers down four points, except the cyc lights and dimmers 25 through 30. Ann, call it after she crosses down right to him." The operation is carried out. The Lighting Designer asks for slight changes, the light levels are adjusted. "Keep that," says the Lighting Designer. "Ann, make that cue 27A." That's how we name inserted cues.

In this fashion, we advance through the script, the Lighting Designer and Scenic Designer solving most of their challenges and problems as they arise, all of the Designers and the Director making notes of things to be worked on later. It takes us two six hour days to get through the show. The Carpenters work alone on the stage for two hours before each run, the Electricians for two hours after. If the actors are not needed on stage, they work with the Director or Choreographer in the theatre's lounge, or go over notes in a dressing room. The authors, of course, are still with us. They, and the Producer, may still be discussing changes—of a word, a line, or a scene.

A short scene is added, requiring a new set, a street lamp and the exterior of the dance hall. The Scenic Designer makes some thumbnail sketches; the Director approves of them. By noon the next day, the Scenic Designer arrives at the theatre with a price from the scenic shop for the additional work. The Producer agrees to the price. The Scenic Designer's Assistant sets to drafting the working drawings. As soon as they are complete, the shop begins to build the new set. The actors are already rehearsing the new scene. In several days, when the set is at the theatre, they will have a chance to work on the new set, while the Lighting Designer cues the new scene. In the next run-through of the show, that scene will be a part of it.

For we do go on running the show. A final technical run-through adds the costumes. We don't stop the action as often this time. The Lighting Designer works with the Electrician and Follow Spot Operators, on headset, during scenes; the Lighting Designer's Assistant takes notes of cues that need changes, and continues to keep an accurate record of the changes as they are made. We stop the rehearsal only to make an involved cue change. The Costume Designer has joined the Director and the other Designers at the Production table. In spare moments the Director confers with him about possible changes. Often, after rehearsal, all of the Designers will meet, with the Stage Managers, Director, Producer and Authors. Schedules and changes are discussed; differences are arbitrated; the next day's work is planned.

ORCHESTRA REHEARSAL, DRESS REHEARSALS AND PREVIEWS

The next to the last people to join the production (the audience are the final, necessary participants in any theatrical event) are the members of the orchestra. Before the dress rehearsal, they assemble in the orchestra pit and with the conductor, play through all of the music in the show. This is the *orchestra readthrough*. A lunch break is taken, and we start our dress rehearsal. All of the elements of the production are involved. The Conductor is likely to stop the run from time to time to make musical adjustments; the rest of us make notes of remaining things to do and things to discuss at the next Production Meeting. The Costume and Lighting Designers discuss any changes they might wish to ask the actors to make in their make-up, which they are wearing at the first time at this rehearsal. The Costume Designer will advise about make-up. For a very complicated make-up effect, such as an elaborate quick change, a *Make-up Consultant* may be hired to design that special make-up. The consultant may be someone associated with a make-up manufacturer, or an experienced film make-up artist.

During the orchestra rehearsal, and later during the run through, the Sound Designer is busy. He adjusts controls on the console, and listens to the sound of the music from various places in the house. Sitting with the Sound Operator, he begins, in the run-through, to set the levels for the controls on the console. More important, he makes sure that the Sound Operator in the house *hears* the way the music should sound. Once the levels are set for the lights, those levels are repeated every night. Indeed they are programmed into the lighting control board's computer, so they will be the same every night. But the quality of the sound can be affected by so many things—the size of the audience, humidity in the air, temperature. Heavy winter coats thrown over seat backs will absorb a great many high tones. Relative sound levels are set, but the Sound Operator must make adjustments each night, so that the sound the audience hears is the sound which the Sound Designer, Director and Composer have agreed on. Since the Sound Operator is seated in the house, he will hear exactly what the audience hears.

There is another full dress rehearsal, with the orchestra and all elements of the production, before we are ready for an audience. Major problems have been solved, and all of the design departments are fine-tuning the show.

Our second week in the theatre, we have preview performances. Tickets are sold to the general public, usually at a reduced price. The production table, of course, has been removed from the theatre, and the Director and Designers will watch the show seated amid the audience, or pacing or skulking at the back of the house. Audience reaction may be a clue to the Producer, Authors, and Director that further changes are called for. Rehearsals may take place during the day; scenes may still be added, changed, or cut. New songs may be put in the show, or new sets.

And then, it's opening night, which is where you came into this whole process.

The increasing number of regional theatres in recent years has brought greater opportunity for jobs, often in attractive, well-equipped quarters. Photo: The Todd Wehr Theater, Performing Arts Center, Milwaukee.

CHAPTER 6

OTHER THEATRE, OTHER JOBS

We have seen that there are literally dozens of artists, craftspeople and support personnel around a particular production for the theatre. But we have been looking at one show on Broadway. Anyone who has lived outside of New York City and who has an interest in the theatre is aware that there are many types of theatres in many cities all over the country. The basic process of putting on a show, however, does not vary that much. The process of preliminary meetings, preparation, design, building, load-in, technical and dress rehearsals is similar in any kind of theatrical activity. Broadway's job structure is the most complex; but in a small dinner theatre in which the design, production organization, building and running of a show may be handled by as few as three people, the same jobs get done. You have, by now, some idea of almost all of the jobs that are involved in putting on a play, but since your first jobs are likely not to be on Broadway, let's try to take a look at some of these other theatrical environments and organizations.

TOURING SHOWS

National Companies

At the time of this writing, the Broadway hit *Annie* has closed in New York. It had run for nearly six years; the creative team which first did the show is preparing a new show entitled *Annie II*. There are, however, four tours of the original *Annie* spread around the country. They may play for as long as six months in a single city, or they may play "one night stands." These shows need people travelling with them other than their casts and dog. They also will hire stage-hands as running crews and to work load-ins and load-outs or "strikes."

There is another type of tour, the "pre-Broadway" or "try-out" tour, in which a new show will schedule performances in one or more major cities before its Broadway opening. Essentially this kind of tour is a series of out-of-town preview performances. All of the initial creative people involved will be with the show as they try to iron out any rough spots in the production before it gets to Broadway. But what types of jobs are available when the producers of a hit show decide to send out a tour while the show is still running on Broadway or immediately after it has closed?

Part of the answer to this question is logical. If the show is a hit in New York and there is also a tour of it, usually called the First National Tour, it stands to reason that the show must be reproduced in its entirety. The number of cast members, the size of the sets, the complexity of certain design elements may be altered to fit each of the theaters that a touring show may play in; alterations may be made in construction methods to insure a quick and efficient load-in and strike; alterations may be made in the materials used in sets and props so that they can withstand the rather heavier wear that frequent set-up, strike and travel entail. But basically, the process and jobs of the personnel necessary to mount the show, to get it ready to tour, is the same as for the original. The trial and error part of the process is done away with, of course. There will be no more re-writes, no more scenes or sets added or cut. The original Costume, Scenic and Lighting Designers are responsible for the design of the Touring Companies, and their Assistants are likely to be very involved in the day-to-day overseeing of details.

Once again at the top of the pyramid of organization is the Production Stage Manager. It might seem that if the show was already complete on Broadway, that there would be less for the P.S.M. to do—less also for the Stage Manager and Assistant. This is hardly the case. Imagine if you were to move everything you own from town to town several times in the course of a few months and you still had to work every day at your job! Not only does the Stage Management team have to deal with the basic running of the show, they must be responsible for making sure that the entire production is travelling with them at all times. People as well as things have a tendency to get lost in strange surroundings. Once again the Stage Managers are responsible for keeping everything and everyone working together.

When a large show goes to various places around the country, there is very little time allotted to set up the show. Advance information about such things as the size of the theatre, the number of dressing rooms, and the space available for storage have been obtained. Advance planning of any adjustments that will have to be made to the sets or lights has been done. But there will always be little problems that must be dealt with on the scene. For that reason, the show will take with it a core group of technicians who are very familiar with the show's needs. Not only will the show need the supervision and job organization of the Stage Management team, it will need the people who can do the physical labor.

Most shows on tour will have a Carpenter and an Assistant Carpenter. Their jobs are to oversee the unloading and unpacking of the scenery at the load-ins. Each piece must be checked to insure its function and usability. As with moving your personal belongings, some pieces get broken. It falls to the Carpenters to maintain and repair any unfortunate pieces of sets. Usually a show on the road has, as part of its workforce, a flyman, whose job it is to supervise all of the rigging and flying of pieces of scenery that travel with a show. A Prop Person, and perhaps an Assistant, travel to oversee and maintain all of the hand properties that are with a show. Perishable food props must be purchased in each location, breakable items may have to be replaced, general maintenance must be kept up.

Most theatres which book National Tours provide only the basic walls, electrical service and rigging which go with the building. A few more recently constructed theaters, including a number of "road houses" on college campuses, may have their own lighting control equipment and an inventory of lighting instruments. In some instances the road show will use this equipment, leaving their own in the truck. More often, the touring company will use its own equipment. It is marked and organized to make the set-up as efficient as possible, and the Electricians are used to working with it. Each tour includes an Electrician and an Assistant who supervise the set-up and strike of all lighting paraphernalia, and who run the show. It also includes a Sound Operator who will make all the necessary arrangements to insure sound of the same quality as the show had in its New York run. The Sound Operator is more likely to use house sound equipment, if there is any in the theatre, since it was designed and installed to compensate for any acoustic problems and eccentricities that that space may have. There is usually very little time to train new personnel on the road, so a tour will have at least one front light operator as a part of its crew. His job will be to run one front light, and to instruct the local crew people who will be operating the other one or two.

As all of the sets, props, lights and sound equipment must be maintained during a tour, so must the costumes and any wigs that the show uses. All shows carry a Costume Mistress or Master, and usually an Assistant for just such a purpose. They also, of course, are responsible for unpacking wardrobe at each stop, and packing it in an organized and efficient fashion at each strike. If a show has a great many wigs, it will also travel with a special person on hand whose job is the care of all the hair pieces.

Finally, since the jobs of all of these people are very important to the success of a show, there must be people who are familiar with the show and each of these jobs. There will be at least one person who is known as the "swing," whose job it is to help in any area that needs it, and to "understudy" the Carpenter, Electrician, Flyman and Sound Operator's running-of-the-show responsibilities.

These dozen or so people are the minimum list of folk who travel with a large show that is on tour. As we have mentioned, there is generally very little time to make the magic happen. In every place that a show stops, there are generally about thirty-five people hired to help with the set-up. Some of these people will function as the running crew once the show opens, and will, no doubt, help in the load-out of the show when it is over.

Bus and Truck Tours

Bus and truck tours are so named because originally the cast rode from theatre to theatre on a bus, while the scenery travelled by truck, with both the bus and the truck, and their drivers, staying with the company for the entire tour. Although the performers may now travel by plane, the scenery is still transported by truck. Scenery for bus and truck tours is frequently "cut down." There is not as much of it, and individual sets are simplified. Some bus and truck tours carry their own lighting equipment, some play only houses that have house equipment available. One of the many responsibilities of the Stage Managers on such a tour is to prepare information sheets to be sent ahead to each theatre with precise technical requirements, and to communicate with the house staffs of these theatres so that, wherever possible, problems can be solved in advance. In addition to the truck driver and the Stage Manager or Stage Managers, such shows may travel with a minimum of three Technicians, usually a Carpenter, Electrician and Wardrobe Master or Mistress. The Electrician or Stage Manager will supervise the Sound set-up, the Carpenter or Stage Manager will oversee Props. Frequently such tours play "split weeks," performing two three-day runs in different cities within the same week, or even "one night stands," in which they play only one performance in each town in which they stop.

Rock Shows. There are, at the present time, a great many rock groups which give concerts on tour. All of them travel with their own sound gear, and therefore with a Sound operator. Often, in addition, there is a person performing some of the functions of a Stage Manager, sometimes called the Production Manager or Technical Supervisor, who oversees the set-up and strike. Some rock shows have extremely elaborate lighting, special effects and wardrobe, and may travel with up to two dozen people to oversee the organization and running of the event. Often they play sports arenas, outdoor stadiums and some unusual facilities, usually for one or two night stands. They travel with all of their lights and staging, and sometimes with portable generators for electrical power. A combination Lighting Designer/Technician is frequently on such tours. The person who is responsible for supervising the lighting set-up will either call the show as a Stage Manager does, or run the lighting control board completely without assistance.

Smaller Tours

Dance Companies.   Some Dance Companies tour with a Carpenter, Electrician, Sound Operator, Wardrobe Attendant and Stage Manager. Some carry only a Stage Manager and one other technician, who divide the preparation duties. Some travel with their own lights, some carry none at all, some plan on using their own equipment only to augment whatever is available in the theatre in which they are playing. Large dance companies travel with drops, cycs and stage curtains, while small troupes carry only a few minimal props and plan to use whatever stage curtains the house has available. The combination Stage Manager/Lighting Designer can frequently find employment with small touring dance companies. If they are lucky, they may not have to drive the truck, too.

Children's Theatre Tours.   In many parts of the country, there are small Children's Theatre companies which tour, very often travelling in a station wagon and a small van. Some of them have a home theatre in which they perform some of the year, taking the same crew and company on the road for brief periods of time. Some of them only tour. Many travel only with a Stage Manager, with the cast helping set-up and strike. Some travel with an additional technician.

Solo Artists and Variety Performers.   The singer who needs only a properly tuned piano, a music stand and a spotlight is likely to travel only with his or her Business Manager, leaving the technical elements of the production to the Manager and the house crew. However, mimes, small one or two person shows with scenery, costumes and props, or any performers who require complicated lighting or scenic effects are likely to travel with a Stage Manager. Again, the Stage Manager/Lighting Designer combination is frequent in this part of the business.

House Crews

No touring company, with the possible exception of the Circus, travels with all of the technical people that it needs to set up and run a show. The touring staff relies on the expertise of local stage crews. Union houses are staffed usually with a Carpenter and an Electrician; some may have larger staffs, employed by the theatre, who are responsible for working or supervising work in all of the attractions that play that house. They, with the local Business Agent, are responsible for hiring the people who help set-up and run touring shows. Non-union houses also have a house staff of some kind. There may be someone whose title is Production Manager or Technical Director, who supervises the use of a particular facility, is in charge of maintenance of the electrical, sound and rigging gear that comprise the house equipment, and is responsible for the hiring and supervision of house crews.

Many colleges host a great many touring events, ranging from lecture series to large scale touring attractions. We cannot overestimate the value of seeking employment as a stagghand in the college "road house," frequently a different facility from the one in which Theatre Department productions take place. You will learn as many ways of organizing and putting a show together as there are companies, you will get a first-hand, hands-on opportunity to study the work of professional Scenic, Lighting and Costume Designers, and you may very likely meet people who will be in a position to help you find employment when you have finished school.

REGIONAL THEATRES

A Regional Theatre is a producing company doing theatre some place other than New York City. Many of them have a Resident Acting Company, some have Resident Designers, and all have people in permanent staff positions in Technical Theatre. This is the first "steady employment" that we have found in the theatre. A group of not-for-profit regional theatres have banded together to form an organization called L.O.R.T., the League of Resident Theatres. Most

Regional Theatres have seasons of from six to ten months, and some truly function year round.

Although the same jobs must be done in order to get a show on in a Regional Theatre as must be done on Broadway, due to the fact that they are permanent producing companies, who always work in the same theatre, and with some continuity of staff from show to show, there are some changes in organization and process.

Two positions not usually found on Broadway exist in Regional Theatres: *Production Manager* and *Technical Director.* The Production Manager's job is to oversee all production related activities of the theatre on a day to day basis. Production Managers generally supervise the scheduling of both people and spaces. They may have some responsibilities dealing with production budgets, or with the purchasing of stage and shop supplies. They trouble-shoot and problem-solve. Since a season may consist of six to twelve shows, the Production Manager is frequently involved in long range planning, while the Stage Manager or Managers (many regional theatres have two Stage Managers, who alternate shows) are concentrating on the details of the show that they are running or rehearsing.

Although some small Regional Theatres have their scenery built by scenic shops, most of them have their own shop facilities. Spaces in which to build and paint sets and props, maintain lighting and sound equipment, build special effects and construct costumes exist, for the exclusive use of the theatre, in the theatre building or near-by spaces. There is also space in which to store sets, props and costumes from previous shows, which may be re-used or rebuilt. The Technical Director coordinates this activity. He or she is responsible for supervising the maintenance and use of the Theatre's equipment. Some Technical Directors seem to concentrate primarily on scenery and rigging, with an Electrician having responsibility for sound and lighting equipment, and a Costumier or Costume Supervisor having responsibility for costume equipment. The Technical Director may also have responsibilities for purchasing supplies and materials. Both the position of Technical Director and that of Production Manager are likely to be defined somewhat differently in each Regional Theatre. Some theatres will have both a Production Manager and a Technical Director; some will have one or the other. For either position, one needs a broad background in all phases of production and design.

Some Regional Theatres have resident staff Costume, Scenic and Lighting Designers. Others may opt to use only Guest Designers, hiring a different design staff for each show. Even with Staff Designers, Guest Designers may be brought in for one or two shows in the season. When Guest Designers are used, the theatre will often have on their staff people who are called Assistants in Design. Their job will be to help the Guest Designers in the completion of their show. Regional Theatres operate within very strict budgets. Particularly since they have storage space available, it makes economic sense to re-use as many elements of scenery and costumes as they can. The job of the Assistants in Design includes informing the Guest Designers of the stock available, and seeing that as much of it as possible is used. In smaller Regional Theatres, the Technical Director and the Costumier or Costume Shop Supervisor will have this responsibility.

Regional Theatres with their own scene shop will employ a Master Carpenter and several Shop Carpenters who will build all of the sets for all of the productions. These people will be hired for their expertise in a variety of areas of set construction. They are likely to be skilled in metal and plastics work as well as woodworking. Their staff may include a Scenic Artist.

Costume Shops are staffed with a Costumier or Shop Supervisor and several stitchers. The Costumier may do pattern cutting, or there may be a separate Cutter. All members of the Costume Staff are likely to have experience in cutting, draping, dying and painting as well as in various construction techniques.

The theatres employ a Property Master or Mistress and usually an Assistant. Their jobs entail finding and building props for the current show, as well as the maintenance of the inventory of props from past shows. The Master Electrician and his or her Assistant are responsible for all electrical equipment, current and past and for future productions. Some theatres employ a worker whose title is Electronics Technician, who specializes in the maintenance of sound equipment and electronic lighting control equipment. This person may also have the responsibility of designing and preparing the sound tapes for shows. In the areas of sound and lights, the theatres keep an inventory of basic equipment, but may build or rent specialized items for particular shows.

Most Regional Theatres have programs for Interns and Apprentices which serve to round out their work forces and to help train young people for a career in the theatre. Some may hire additional workers in the scenic or costume shop where there is a particularly heavy work load. Each theatre is almost entirely different in its needs and consequent staffing. Some theatres may employ a Resident Scenic Artist; others may expect Scenic Designers to paint their own sets, or require the Technical Director to have a good knowledge of scenic painting. A theatre without a Sound Designer on its staff may have show sound done by an Electrician, a Stage Manager, the Technical Director, or an outside sound studio. The theatres each have a different approach to staffing, based on their budgets and needs, and on the skills and interests of their staff members. Research into the actual structure of an individual theatre will help you gain knowledge of the kinds of positions they are likely to have available.

DINNER THEATRES

Dinner theatres are perhaps a sub-category of Regional Theatres. Tables and restaurant seating make up the audience area, and admission most often includes both a meal and the show. They vary tremendously in size, from very small installations, doing small–cast straight plays to large elaborate installations specializing in musicals. Their shows run from three to six weeks each. Some have their own shops, while some have their scenery built by an outside shop. Most hire their Designers by the job. All have Stage Managers and Lighting Operators. Again, the Stage Manager/Lighting Designer combination is popular. Scene shifts may be "staged" and done by actors, or by employees who also act as waiters and busboys.

SUMMER THEATRES

Summer Theatres could be defined as seasonal Regional Theatres. They exist all over the country; New England, New York State, and

Pennsylvania are virtually peppered with them. They vary greatly in the size of their operations and their staffs. There are huge, outdoor, star-oriented theatres, such as the Municipal Opera in St. Louis, which employ dozens of highly skilled union members. There are also small non-Equity theatres, all of whose technical and design work is done by their acting companies. And there are all of the possible steps between. The majority of Summer Theatres do not use union crews. All of them have their own shop facilities, some extremely well-equipped, some very primitive. Some manage to mount a different show each week, some do shows for two or three week runs. Some mostly or exclusively accommodate summer touring shows, which do not, however, usually tour with their scenery. Sets are built and lighting is designed at each of the theatres on the tour, based on floor plans and general descriptions received from the tour manager. A minimum Summer Theatre staff will consist of a Stage Manager, Costume Designer, one person who designs Scenery and Lighting, and a Technical Director, who will be assisted by the Apprentices. Larger operations will include on their staffs one or more Assistant Stage Managers, a Properties Person, an Electrician, separate Designers for Scenery and Lighting, a Scenic Artist, several Carpenters, a Wardrobe staff of from one to four and a Sound Designer. Some of these positions, at a minimal salary, may be assigned to qualified Apprentices or Interns.

A specialized kind of Summer Theatre is the Outdoor Pageant. Mostly located in the South, they perform the same show all summer, year after year. The shows are often based on some regional historical person or event. Their casts may include horses and burros as well as over a hundred actors. Sets and costumes are repeated from year to year, albeit rebuilt and refurbished. Outdoor Pageants employ a large complement of technicians.

UNIVERSITY THEATRE

Design positions in colleges and universities are most often filled by faculty members who also have teaching responsibilities. Some

Designers find that they can teach, design the school shows that are a part of their contract, and still find time for outside professional Design work. One year contracts, to replace a faculty member on sabbatical leave, are sometimes available. These will always involve teaching. Some universities and colleges may hire an outside Designer for a single show. This is usually done under a "guest artist contract." If the guest artist is not required to teach any classes, he or she will probably be asked to conduct a series of informal seminars or critique sessions with advanced students.

University and college theatres employ Stage Managers only if they have a professional L.O.R.T. company affiliated with them. However, university and college theatre is an expanding job place for theatre technicians. Colleges often employ from one to six theatre technicians, responsible for building sets, props and costumes, overseeing student crews and maintaining equipment. Job titles include Technical Director, Carpentry Shop Foreman or Master Carpenter, House Electrician, Costume Shop Foreman, Cutter, Stitcher, electronics Maintenance Person. Practical experience in the field is as important a pre-requisite for such a position as educational credits. Unlike most other jobs in the theatre, work in university and college theatre affords steady, secure employment.

COMMUNITY THEATRE

The thousands of Community Theatres throughout the country are primarily recreational, leisure-time activities, with few paid positions. They are exceptionally fine places for young Designers and technicians, even those in high school, to gain experience. They afford an opportunity for people contemplating career changes to "try out" the field of theatre. The few established Community Theatres which do employ a professional staff may have a Wardrobe Supervisor and a Technical Director or Master Carpenter. If they use Designers who are other than members of the group, they are jobbed in for a single show.

OTHER THEATRE JOBS

The U.S. Army.   The Army's Morale Support Program employs a number of civilian Theatre Specialists. Their activities and responsibilities vary with the specific post and assignment. Sometimes they must direct plays as well as supervise Design and building. In all cases they function as Production Manager.

Opera.   The few Opera Companies in the country with long seasons employ a large number of union stagehands, both in their shops and running shows. Because they work "in repertory," changing from one show to another daily during their seasons, they usually employ a Resident Lighting Designer. New stage settings are individually commissioned from Designers of repute, world wide. Perhaps the greatest responsibility of the Opera Stage Manager is supervising rehearsals after opening, when the Stage Director is no longer in residence. Small Opera Companies abound; most of them hire their Designers and technicians on a show to show basis.

Circus.   Yes, the Circus travels with stagehands; Electricians, Riggers, Carpenters and Welders. Living quarters and meals are supplied on the Circus train.

Nightclubs.   Many Nightclubs employ a technician whose responsibility is running lights and sound for their attractions. Elaborate Night Club installations, such as those found in Atlantic City and Las Vegas, possess highly sophisticated electronic systems which control curtains, turntables and other scenic elements as well as lights and sound. They do offer employment for skilled stagehands and for Wardrobe Attendants adept at sewing on sequins.

Industrial Shows.   Large manufacturing firms frequently present their new product lines to salesmen and dealers in a theatrical fashion at annual conventions. Sometimes these presentations are elaborate multimedia shows with films and slides; sometimes they are full scale musical productions with many performers, many sets and many costumes. The fashion shows at which clothing designers and manufacturers introduce their new lines to retailers frequently involve lavish scenic backgrounds, lighting effects and technicians to make them happen.

Theme Parks.   A final source of employment is in Theme Parks, amusement parks built around an idea. Most of the larger Theme Parks present concerts, strolling bands, variety shows and other forms of live entertainment. They therefore have a need for technicians, stagehands and wardrobe people. Most Theme Parks operate only in the summer. Salaries range from $140 to $300 per week. A list of Theme Park contacts is included in the Appendix.

THEATRE-RELATED JOBS

Although most employment in the theatre is directly related to putting on shows, there are some theatre-related careers not directly involved with production.

Industry

There are a great many firms throughout the country which manufacture, sell and rent lighting, sound, costume and special effects equipment. A majority of their sales and engineering personnel have a background which includes theatre training and experience. The most common theatrical supplier is the "general theatre house," which sells and rents lighting, sound and intercom equipment, sells make-up and may supply stage curtains and rigging, costume and scenic fabrics and special effects devices. A great deal of their service is problem-solving for a customer. Sales personnel are expected to know which particular pieces of equipment will best solve a particular production problem. Both the companies and the customers are more secure with workers who have had actual production training and experience. Some young Designers and Technicians can combine a day time job with a theatrical supplier and evening production work in Community Theatre or Showcase productions. Some manufacturing firms offer internships to students (See Chapter 9), which may result in full time employment upon graduation. Technicians who are attracted to a career in the design or development of lighting and sound equipment should consider advanced education with a concentration in engineering,optics, acoustics or computer technology.

Scene crew members at the Lyric Opera House plan moves for the many drops necessary in opera production. Photo: Lyric Opera of Chicago.

Teaching

There are many opportunities available teaching theatre. For some it is their only job; some Designers, Technicians and Stage Managers located near the production centers of New York, Chicago and Los Angeles both teach and work at an independent career in the theatre; others teach for nine months of the year and look forward to a Summer Theatre job for the remaining time. An M.F.A. or Ph.D is virtually a necessity for college or university teaching, although graduate assistantships or positions as Instructor may be available for those who are finishing their terminal degree. In some community colleges or small liberal arts colleges, a teacher of theatre design or technology will be expected to teach other art, theatre or speech courses.

Some large high schools have well-staffed theatre departments, and include teachers whose only responsibilities are in theatre design and production; in many high schools the theatre department is one person who directs the plays and teaches a general theatre course in addition to being responsible for design. A high school theatre teacher may combine theatre expertise with teaching English, Art, or indeed, any other subject in which he or she is certified in the state in which they are teaching. Most states do not have separate secondary school teacher certification in theatre; some do. Inquiry should be made to the Department of Education in the state in which you wish to teach. Finally, positions are available supervising the theatrical activity of elementary schools, and working with children in school-sponsored children's theatre. Some of these positions involve directing as well as designing.

Commercial Design and Display

Several areas of design and display work are open to an individual with theatre training. Designers and prop makers may find themselves particularly attracted to store window display. Most large department stores have display departments with from two to a dozen employees. They are usually responsible for in-store displays as well as windows, and both plan and execute them. Firms known as *display houses* contract for display work for large conventions, festivals, parade floats and special advertising campaigns.

As some people come to the field of theatre design through an interest in interior design, so can theatre Designers find work as interior designers. Boutiques and restaurants seeking a very special, dramatic setting seem most interested in having their spaces dressed by someone with stage experience.

Within the past decade, the field of Architectural Lighting Design has become very important. Proper lighting of all public space and work space is necessary to health, safety, comfort and productivity. Many theatrically trained Lighting Designers, already aware of the nature and uses of light, have acquired a familiarity with architectural lighting equipment and the additional expertise that will enable them to specify the lighting for factories, convention centers, restaurants, museums and office buildings.

Theatre Consulting

Background and training in all phases of theatre technology and design, an interest in and familiarity with theatrical equipment, and a fascination with the process of making theatre and the spaces in which theatre is made are requirements of a theatre consultant. Although sales personnel in theatre houses may work with theatre owners describing and making recommendations about types of equipment and materials to use in small theatre remodellings and renovations, most builders of new theatres employ a Theatre Consultant, who works with both the architect and the owner of the building, to plan, for that theatre and the activity which will take place in it, the most efficient use of space and the appropriate specifications of its equipment. There are perhaps a dozen firms in the country, with from one to several dozen employees, which devote themselves to this kind of work.

Careful union regulations govern the responsibilities of every category of worker in productions in various classifications of theaters. Photos: above, The Cleveland Play House; below, publications from Actors Equity, United Scenic Artists, International Ladies Garment Workers Union, and the International Alliance of Theatrical Stage Employees and Moving Picture Machine Operators.

CHAPTER 7

UNIONS

Unions, to a greater or lesser degree, are a part of all professional theatrical activity. At the present time, all of the people involved in running a show on Broadway must have a union contract. All of the materials used in a Broadway show, with the exception of stage properties purchased or rented on the open market and costume items purchased in the same fashion, must originate from a union shop. As a Broadway theatre production is the most elaborate theatrical organization, so is it the most highly unionized. The personnel of a first class tour are similarly all union members. Bus and truck tours travel with one or two union Stage Managers and from one to six union technicians. The lighting and sound technicians who tour with rock shows, musical attractions and large dance companies are most often union members. All shows whose casts are members of Actors' Equity Association must have at least one union Stage Manager. The technicians travelling with childrens' theatre tours, small dance companies and most "one man shows" are usually not union members.

The staffs of L.O.R.T. theatres vary in their union affiliation from a full complement of union workers to a Stage Manager's being the only union-affiliated design or technical employee.

The house crews of the theatres in which touring attractions perform may be entirely, partially, or not at all staffed by union members. The road show presentation houses in many large colleges often have union crews, with whom student non-union members may work, by permit, gaining valuable experience.

Although there are people who have no union affiliation earning their living in the theatre, it is likely that union membership will figure into your theatrical career. Certainly a consideration of it is necessary.

All union agreements establish minimum salaries and wages for various kinds of work that fall under their jurisdiction. What are described as "union rules" are actually contractual obligations. The terms of each class of contract are negotiated by the unions and such representatives of management as the League of New York Theatres (for everyone on Broadway), the League of Resident Theatres (for regional theatres affiliated with that organization); or by the unions and individual management of scenic, lighting, sound and costume shops, and sometimes by the unions and the management of individual theaters. By signing a union contract, both producer and union member agree to abide by its terms and to do nothing contrary to those terms.

In addition to salary and wages, union contracts are concerned with working hours, compensation for overtime, the payment of travel and *per diem* expenses (living expenses out of town), scheduling of time off, dinner breaks, rest periods, and the insurance of safe and sanitary working conditions. Designers' contracts describe the terms under which the designs may be used in future productions of the show. The duties and job of the Stage Manager, Designer or Stage Technician are described in Union "rule" books; the satisfactory accomplishment of that job becomes the worker's contractual obligation.

I.A.T.S.E.

The oldest of the theatrical unions is the International Alliance of Theatrical Stage Employees, shortened conversationally to "the I.A." or "yat-see" or "the stagehands union." Its members are stage carpenters, property people, electricians, sound operators and wardrobe workers. Some union members work in only one department, some in several. The union itself establishes no distinction between carpenters, electricians, flymen and properties persons; a member of the

I.A. may be hired in any capacity. Contracts are issued for "carpenters," "electricians," "sound operators" and "properties persons." Some sound designers and special effects specialists belong to an affiliate of the I.A. known as the Associated Crafts. Wardrobe Attendants comprise another I.A. Affiliate. Another branch of this union, a branch outside of our immediate subject, is made up of Motion Picture Projectionists. Some major cities have other branches for film workers, cutters and editors as well as grips (carpenters) and gaffers (electricians) and make-up and hair stylists. In most large cities the projectionists and theatre workers belong to separate *locals,* the organization of I.A. members in that area. A few of these cities have separate locals for Wardrobe Attendants. If a separate Wardrobe Attendants Local does not exist, the wardrobe workers are members of the Theatrical Local.

In smaller towns, the I.A. members are formed into what is known as a mixed local, comprised of both projectionists and stage workers, including wardrobe attendants.

The international headquarters of the I.A. is located at 1515 Broadway, New York, NY 10036. Theatrical workers are a part of locals in all fifty states and Canada. Touring and Production Contracts are handled through the International. Other jobs on Broadway, house and running crew positions, are handled by Local #1, the New York City local. Jobs on load-in, load-outs and running touring shows are handled through the locals in each town or area the show plays. Minimum salaries are established by the International, but the individual locals have a great deal of autonomy, and may establish practices concerning hours, safety and working conditions for their particular jurisdictions. The locals function as hiring halls, something not true of the other theatrical unions. The International provides members with medical insurance. This medical plan may be augmented by the locals. Some, but far from all of the locals have Pension Plans. Locals negotiate with scenic, lighting and sound shops in their area concerning such matters as salary, vacation pay and pension and welfare benefits. Each shop is assigned a shop number, which must be displayed, at the center of a union label, on each piece of scenery or equipment constructed or prepared by the shop. This union "bug" is stencilled on the backs of scenic units, and applied as a sticker to lighting and sound equipment.

How Do You Join the I.A.?

The easiest way to become a member of the I.A. is to be the son or daughter of an I.A. member, but that is not the only way. Some locals have established apprentice programs, with admission by periodically administered examinations. All locals will, from time to time, accept new members on the basis of experience. If a local does not have enough members available to fill the "call" for a particular job, non-union technicians may work by permit. Frequently, such permits may be issued to theatre students at a local college, and sometimes new union members are drawn from the ranks of these "permittees." People have first become affiliated with the I.A. in New York City, but it is easier to secure union membership in a less crowded local. The I.A. is very concerned about keeping a maximum number of their members working. They do not want many times more members than there are jobs available. Some technicians persue union membership for several years before joining the I.A.

About Women.   In the early 1970's, the authors knew of only two women I.A. members working in theatre who were not Wardrobe Attendants. This is no longer true. The I.A. has female members who work in all areas. Not all locals have moved in this direction; some of these locals, however, have been kept from enrolling any new members by a lack of work in their area. The absorption of women workers into a traditionally male world has, once it got started, proceeded at a greater pace than that of many other male dominated occupations.

THE I.L.G.W.U.

The only work in technical theatre (excluding Design and Stage Managing) not covered by the I.A. is that of stitchers in costume shops. Like other workers in the "needle trades," they are represented by the International Ladies Garment Workers Union. The I.L.G.W.U.'s jurisdiction includes some large costume shops affiliated with a single theatre (the Metropolitan Opera and Radio City Music Hall shops in New York City) as well as independent shops. Unlike most other theatrical unions, union membership is not a requirement of initial employment. After you have been hired by a union costume shop and worked there for thirty days, you must join the I.L.G.W.U., which sets minimum wages, hours and working conditions, and provides pension and welfare benefits.

STAGE MANAGERS

Stage Managers are members of Actors' Equity Association. Equity has only one class of membership. Equity contracts specify minimum wages for Stage Managers which differ from those of actors; they also concern themselves with specific duties, responsibilities and protection for Stage Managers. But the union does not have a separate Stage Management branch or local. People who stage manage can, and do, perform as actors. The authors, both Stage Managers, find it very important for even the most single-minded Stage Manager to have acted at some time during his or her career. Acting provides a working understanding of the process and the language which actors use, and a familiarity with the problems and temperaments peculiar to performers.

Persons contracted as Production Stage Managers or Stage Managers cannot understudy or perform in a show in which they are so contracted. Assistant Stage Managers can, and frequently do, act as understudies and perform in small roles. Experience as a performer may cause a person to be hired as an Assistant Stage Manager over someone without that experience.

Actors' Equity Association, referred to as "Equity," is a national union. It does not have locals, although it does maintain regional offices in San Francisco, Los Angeles and Chicago. Its National Headquarters are located at 1540 Broadway, New York, NY 10036. There are area-liaison people in Atlanta, Miami, Boston and St. Louis. W.A.B. and M.A.B., the Western Advisory Board and Midwest Advisory Board meet regularly to deal with local matters, but all executive decisions on union affairs are made by Equity Council, a non-salaried governing board comprised entirely of working members of the union.

Equity provides its members with Medical Insurance and has a minimal Dental Insurance Plan and a Pension Plan. Vacation pay accrues to Equity members working for 13 weeks or more under the same contract. Producers must arrange for Equity members to be covered by unemployment insurance in the state in which the member is resident.

Equity has contracts covering Stage Managers for Broadway, off-Broadway, in touring productions, summer stock theatres, dinner theatres, L.O.R.T. theatres and cabaret theatres as well as Letters of Agreement with developing theatres (theatres beginning operation, hoping to work their way up to full Equity status). Every Equity production must have an Equity Stage Manager. Some contracts demand an Assistant Stage Manager. Stage Managers for Equity-Approved Funded Theatre ("showcase") productions in New York and 99-seat Waiver productions on the West Coast may be either Equity or non-Equity.

HOW DO YOU BECOME A MEMBER OF EQUITY?

Equity, of all the theatrical unions, is the easiest to affiliate with. This does not seem to be the case to a young Stage Manager starting out, stuck in the "Catch-22" enigma of not being able to join the union without having an Equity contract, but not being able to acquire an Equity contract without being a member of Equity. People do join the union by being awarded an Equity contract: a producer may decide to move a successful showcase or non-Equity production to Equity status, or a producer or Stage Manager with whom you have worked in some capacity in a showcase, summer stock or L.O.R.T. theatre may decide that you are the Assistant Stage Manager they need for a particular production.

There is another, more traditional route to Equity membership. The E.M.C. (Equity Membership Candidate) programs are operated in L.O.R.T. Theatres, dinner theatres, Chicago off-Loop theatres and summer theatres. Acceptance into the program is most often by audition and interview at the participating theatre. Some, but not all summer theatre apprentices are eligible to be Equity Membership

Candidates. Once a person has been accepted into an E.M.C. program, he or she writes to Actors' Equity Association, requesting an E.M.C. enrollment form. It is to be filled out and returned to Equity with a one time payment of $50. The payment covers the clerical work necessary for keeping records of your work as an E.M.C. The amount is deductible from your initiation fee when you join the union.

Your enrollment as an E.M.C. is good for a five year period. E.M.C.s work as actors or Stage Management interns for 50 weeks. Crew work alone may be performed for some few of those weeks, but for the majority of your E.M.C. candidacy you must be listed in the program as performing, understudying or assisting the Stage Manager. After completing 50 weeks of work (not necessarily all at the same theatre, that's why the record-keeping gets complicated), the E.M.C. may, upon payment of an initiation fee ($500 in 1983) and dues for the current six months, become a member of Equity. Base Equity dues are $52 per year, half payable in May and November. Additional dues payments, 2% of a member's weekly salary, are deducted by management each week he or she works under contract, and forwarded to the union.

After completing the maximum 50 week's work, a person may no longer be hired as an E.M.C. An E.M.C. may, upon application to Equity after having amassed 30 weeks of E.M.C. credit, take a written test, objective questions dealing with the union's rules and history. If the candidate passes the exam, he or she may join Equity at that time.

When Should You Join Equity?

Once a person is a member of Actors' Equity Association, he or she can never again act or Stage Manage in a non-Equity production. All of his or her work as actor or Stage Manager must be covered by an Equity Contract, Code, Waiver or Letter of Agreement. This restriction is much sharper for Equity members than for stagehands, who under some circumstances may work in non-union shops; or for Designers, whose union does not, at this time, have standard contracts for some types of theatrical production. The only exception to this rule is for regularly enrolled students in a theatre program, who may, while they are students, participate in school productions. A Costume, Lighting or Scenic designer who is a member of United Scenic Artists may design a show for a community theatre. Even if given the opportunity, an Equity Stage Manager cannot stage manage that community theatre show. Affiliating with Equity before you have gained a substantial body of experience is an easy way to become a non-working Equity Stage Manager. Separate statistics are not available for Stage Managers, but at any given time 85% of the members of A.E.A. are not at work anywhere under an Equity contract. By joining the union before one is adequately prepared, one is likely to become frequently a part of the theatrically-unemployed.

THE UNITED SCENIC ARTISTS

Scenic Painters, designers of scenery, lighting and costumes, and their assistants are members of United Scenic Artists, an affiliate of the Brotherhood of Painters and Allied Trades. U.S.A. has two locals, 829 in New York and 350 in Chicago. If a production originates in California and the designer is not a member of 829 or 350, he or she must be a member of Los Angeles I.A. local 816. Locals 829 and 350 are autonomous; their rules are somewhat different, but not their overall procedure for joining.

There is a negotiated agreement between the U.S.A. and the League of New York Theatres; designers for Broadway shows must be members of U.S.A. There are negotiated agreements with a number of scenic shops; all scenery on Broadway has been painted by members of U.S.A. Nowhere else in theatres does this absolutely closed shop exist; non-union Designers may work off-Broadway and in stock and regional theatres. In practice, the great majority of working Designers have union affiliation. U.S.A. covers design work in the above areas and in opera and ballet, as well as film, television and commercials. As with Actors' Equity Association, work by a U.S.A. member in an area not covered by a union contract must be covered by a Letter of Agreement.

The U.S.A. establishes minimum wages, royalty payments for

Broadway work, travel and *per diem* expenses and subsequent use of the designs by another company or production. Their contract with scenic shops include stipulations about overtime, meal breaks, holidays and paid vacations. Union benefits include Medical Insurance, Dental Insurance, Life Insurance, a Pension Fund, a Sick and Benefit Fund and Death Benefits. The U.S.A. sometimes functions as a hiring hall, mostly for Scenic Artists. Salaries for Scenic Artists, in 1983 in New York, ranged from $800 to $1000 a week. Minimum Fees for Broadway Designers for plays begin at around $2000 for Costumes and Lighting, and at around $3500 for Sets. The minimums increase with the number of scenes in the show (for Scenic and Lighting Designers) or the number of characters (for Costume Designers). Minimums are higher for musicals than for plays. In Regional Theatre and off-Broadway, salaries are scaled by the seating capacity of the theatre as well as by the size of the show. Minimums for large regional theatres are about half of the Broadway fees. Fees for small (199 seats or less) off-Broadway and Regional Theatres begin at $570. Designers may, of course, negotiate fees that are greater than the minimums. They are also likely to spend from two to six months working on and overseeing the designs for an individual show.

Categories of membership in the U.S.A. include

1. Scenic Artist
2. Scenic Designer and Art Director
3. Costume Designer
4. Lighting Designer
5. Allied Crafts (craftspersons and prop makers)

Industrial Member is a sub-category of Scenic Artist, and is made up of Shop Men (who may be women), the people who mix paints and clean and care for equipment. The U.S.A. has recently begun an apprentice program in the Scenic Artist category. The union also has two non-theatrical categories of membership, Mural Artist and Diorama, Model and Display Maker.

Dues for the five categories listed above are quarterly payments of $34.50 plus 2% of monies earned under the union's jurisdiction. Dues for Industrial Members are less.

How Do You Become a Member of the United Scenic Artists?

Both Local 829 and Local 350 give examinations in late spring. Passing the exam is the most common route to Union membership. The U.S.A. Union Examination is the Theatrical Design equivalent to the certification examinations taken by doctors, lawyers and architects.

To take the exam, you write the union, requesting an application form. This must be filled out and returned to them, with a $50 registration fee. You will receive a letter back describing a home project, to be worked on during the three or four weeks before your interview, the next step in the process. The exact nature of the exam varies from year to year. The home project is likely to involve reading a specific play, opera, novel or scenario and doing whatever background research you think might be necessary. They may request a model, or complete drafting, rendering and working drawings of one or more scenes. Scenic Artist's take-home projects will involve several techniques of scene painting. You will be given about a month to finish the take home project or research, which you will bring with you to your interview.

You are expected to bring with you to the interview for the exam a resume listing your design work and a portfolio with examples of your work, drafting, renderings and photographs, as well as your home project. (We will describe the process of putting together a resume and portfolio in Chapter 9).

A committee of U.S.A. members will examine both your home project and your other work at the interview. They may ask you questions about your design concept, and ask you to explain details of drafting and construction. In some cases, you will be advised by the examination committee not to take the exam this year. They may even suggest areas in which you need more work or study. The interview and discussion of the home project is the first phase of the exam. If you are accepted for the next step, you will be charged the balance of the examination fee, from $50 to $115.

Costume, Scenic and Lighting Designers arrive at the examination place laden with drawing boards, paints, brushes, drafting materials and lunch. They will be given several projects to complete. They may be asked to design elements of the assigned work that were not included in the home project, or to redesign elements of it for a larger or smaller scaled production, or for film or television rather than the stage. The Costume and Lighting Designers may be asked to prepare shop orders as well. Scenic Designers should be expected to both paint and draft. Lighting Designers, in addition to their day at the drawing board, will be scheduled for a practical examination. It will take place in a theatre which has a minimal set, lights and an I.A. crew. The Lighting Designers are given several design problems to solve, while a union committee observes. The Designers are judged both on the quality of their design solutions and the ease and efficiency with which they work with the Electricians. The exam for Scenic Artists is held at a scenic studio, and involves reproducing full scale on a 6' x 8' canvas a painting or Designer's elevation.

The work is graded individually by each member of a group of judges and these results are averaged. In about eight weeks you will be told if you were successful. If you have passed the exam, you will, after having been voted on by the membership, and upon the payment of an initiation fee of $1000 for Scenic Designers and Scenic Artists and $500 for Costume and Lighting Designers, be initiated into the U.S.A. Most people who take the exam do not pass it the first year they take it.

It is possible to be taken into the union without taking the exam, if a Producer insists on your designing his or her Broadway show. Although this has happened on occasion, when a play or musical has moved from a regional or off-Broadway theatre to Broadway, it is infrequent. In this case, you must apply to the U.S.A. for membership, be voted upon by the members, and pay professional initiation fees of $2500 for Scenic Designers and Scenic Artists and $2000 for Costume and Lighting Designers.

The sound operator using the control board during a college production is
in touch with others backstage and in the house through her headset.
Photo: NTC.

CHAPTER 8

EDUCATION

Preparation for a career in Theatrical Design and Production should involve a combination of study and practical experience. It requires some training in specific theatrical techniques (scenic construction, property making, costume painting, production organization); in generalized design and technical theory and practice (rendering, drafting, optics, physics and engineering) and, since the subject matter of most theatre pieces is real or fantasized human experience, in a solid background in the humanities (history, art history, psychology, languages and literature). Almost all of the colleges in the country have some theatre courses, in English Departments, Theatre Departments, or in separate Schools of Speech, Arts, or Communication. All of them have some kind of a production program.

WHAT KIND OF PROGRAMS ARE OFFERED IN DESIGN AND TECHNICAL THEATRE?

The Associate of the Arts Certificate (A.A.)

This is a two year program offered by some junior colleges, and by some vocationally-oriented four year colleges. The program's aim is the training of qualified, capable theatre technicians, and therefore can be regarded as a terminal degree. However, many graduates of such a program go on to complete a B.A., B.F.A. or further to graduate work. The program involves a minimum of liberal arts courses; if you go on to a four year program from an A.A. program, a large portion of your last two years will be spent fulfilling liberal arts requirements. Such programs, however, often have more than usually extensive job placement services. It may be possible, with an A.A. certificate, to support the continuation of your education by working in the theatre. Some A.A. programs have established a relationship with an I.A. apprenticeship program; many A.A. programs have working theatre professionals as instructors. Perhaps the oldest such program in the country, and one very proud of its many working graduates, is Los Angeles City College, Los Angeles, CA.

Four Year Colleges

Degrees offered are B.A. (Bachelor of Arts), B.S. (Bachelor of Science) and B.F.A. (Bachelor of Fine Arts). The B.F.A. puts a greater focus on practical work, frequently demanding the design, stage management or technical direction of a major production as a degree requirement. B.A. and B.S. degrees are frequently in Theatre, rather than in Scenic Design or Stage Management, but there is some specialization allowed. B.F.A. programs are frequently offered with concentration in Design (sometimes with a specialization in Lighting, Scenic or Costume Design) and sometimes have a specialization in Theatre Technology.

Graduate Programs

Degrees offered are M.A. and M.F.A. Like the B.F.A., the Master of Fine Arts is a more professionally oriented program. An M.F.A. thesis almost always involves a major design or production project; an M.A. thesis tends to be scholarly research. A Ph.D. is available from many universities in Theatre; most of the holders of such degrees teach at the college level.

A Professional Training School

Unique among theatre training places is the Studio and Forum of Stage Design, 727 Washington Street, New York, NY 10014. It offers two and three year Certificate programs in scenic design, costume design and lighting design. Its staff are working designers and crafts-people; courses include scene painting, model making and mask and prop making, as well as design techniques, drawing and painting, theatre history and research. One may either enroll in the two or three year program, or elect to take one or more specific courses.

CHOOSING A COLLEGE OR UNIVERSITY

Classroom lectures are only a part of a college education in theatre. Since some of your most valuable college experience will be working on the production of plays, we strongly recommend that, if at all possible, you make a visit to the campus of any school that you are considering. Look at the facilities that are available. If there is only one performance space, there will not be as much production going on as there will if there are several. What is the ratio of teachers to students? In design particularly, individualized attention from a pro-fessor is important. How great are the opportunities for students to design and stage manage? Are there many opportunities, or will most of your work be classroom "paper projects?" Does the school have its own Summer Theatre, or a L.O.R.T. theatre on campus or located near-by? Are there courses available in non-theatre subjects which are important to the development of your theatrical career? Courses in Applied Physics or Electrical Engineering are important to future Sound Operators, Technical Directors and designers of lighting equip-ment. Courses in Applied Art and Art History are important to would-be Designers. Try to locate recent graduates of a school in which you are interested, to get their perspectives on it. If you are still in high school, your sophomore year is not too early to begin collecting information about possible colleges.

Although it is out of print as this is being written, the American Theatre Association (see Appendix B) publishes a *Directory of American College Theatre.* Your library may have a copy. It provides, in efficient, tabular form, information about a great many college and university theatre programs.

Almost all state universities have well-developed programs in

Students at a Columbia College Chicago work on the set of a major department production. Photos: Teresa Poling.

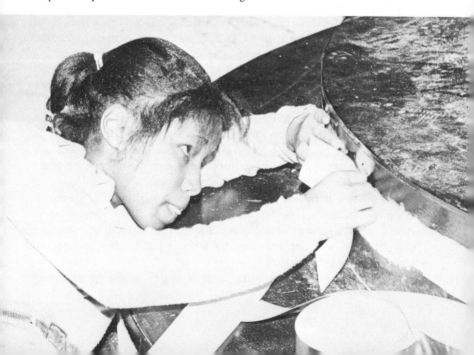

theatre design and technology. The Universities of California, Illinois, Indiana, Iowa, Massachusetts, Minnesota, Texas and Wisconsin have a nation-wide reputation in this area, as do Pennsylvania State University and the various campuses of the State University of New York. Among city institutions, New York University, Boston University and San Diego State University have extensive programs. Well known private universities include Purdue, Carnegie-Mellon and Webster University in St. Louis. Ithaca College in Ithaca, New York has a very professionally oriented program. Yale, which has only a graduate program in Theatre, is the alma mater of a great many working Designers and Technicians. There are two schools in the country which specialize in training in the arts. California Institute of the Arts and North Carolina School of the Arts have very professionally aimed programs. Their cross-disciplinary structure affords the theatre student an opportunity to work in opera and ballet as well as drama. Ohio State University has a program in Design for Dance; Indiana University's School of Music houses a Department of Design for Musical Theatre, as does the Cincinnati College Conservatory of Music.

Intermission at The Little Theatre On the Square, summer theatre in Sullivan, Illinois. Producer Jean Webster is at far right.

CHAPTER 9

GETTING STARTED

Anyone who has been working in theatre for more than about one hour has probably been asked "How did you get started?" It is a favorite question of talk show hosts, students, apprentices, working Stage Managers, Broadway Designers, and Tony Award winners. If you were to listen to the answers that one hundred people gave, the great majority of the answers would boil down to "I just sort of started. I did a great many jobs along the way, and one morning, woke up and found myself here." This answer is as true as it can be, and there is a key in the phrasing "a great many jobs along the way." We must all begin somewhere, and most of us began the day we decided to try a life of theatre job-hunting, with all its rewards and disappointments. It may have been the day in school when we found ourselves on the light crew and not cast in the lead of the play. It may have been the day we volunteered to move scenery in the local little theatre play. Eventually, we found ourselves looking for broader horizons and experience, with, one hopes, a bit of salary thrown in for good measure. Once we have decided to climb the long ladder to the life of professional theatre, we are faced with "how to begin?"

To begin, we must look at what jobs there are available, how to find out about them, and what is needed to apply for them. First, what jobs are there?

A great many people begin as a Summer Theatre apprentice, the entry level position in most Summer Theatres. "Apprentice" has a multitude of meanings, all of which boil down to long, hard work, with little, if any, pay. As mentioned earlier in this book, Summer

Theatres are generally understaffed and overworked organizations. In some theatres, which often have a full program of classes and productions for apprentices, there is a fee charged to apprentices. It often includes room and board, and may be as much as $2000 for the summer. At other theatres, there is no fee and no payment. Some of these will supply living quarters and kitchen facilities or meals. Some theatres do pay apprentices, but the pay is always barely enough to live on, often as little as $25 to $50 per week. Often this stipend is considered only for a very few "on scholarship." Probably the best way to decide on the course for you is to compile information about the programs of various theatres and decide what you hope to gain during the summer. Then apply where you feel would benefit you the most. Remember that to apply to one or only a few of the myriad of theatres is to risk total rejection. There are few theatres in comparison to the large number of people seeking jobs. The more contacts you make, the higher are your chances of being accepted. Don't wait until the summer to apply to these theatres. Most places begin looking for summer workers in January and February. It takes a great deal of time to process all of the applications that a theatre receives and a great deal of time to make decisions as to the staff they will need. Be sure, if you are in school, to keep a sharp eye on the departmental bulletin board after the first of the year. Summer Theatres, especially those with apprentice programs, will send announcements to colleges. This information is likely to be posted, and will explain the required application procedure for each theatre. Often, a college or university either runs its own summer program, or is closely affiliated with a Summer Theatre. Information on the availability of positions at their theatre will, of course, be posted in your department. There are other sources to be explored, which will be explained later in this chapter.

L.O.R.T.

The position of apprentice is obviously the low end of the theatrical chain of command. An apprentice often functions as a theatre's main source of labor, working extremely long hours for very short pay. The person who serves that function in a L.O.R.T. Theatre is often called an intern. There are some major differences and major benefits to be gained from working for L.O.R.T. Theatres.

Generally, Summer Theatres operate from 10 to 14 weeks per year, while most L.O.R.T. theatres operate on at least a 6 month or 26 week season. Often they have seasons as long as ten months. What this means is that the staff has more of an opportunity to begin truly to function as a production team—or family. They find themselves with a bit more leisure during the production period for each show. They often, therefore, can spend more time on intensive training for the interns, with classes and individual instruction. Since a summer operation has little time for learning by error, you may find yourself only observing some projects, not getting the opportunity to do the work and sufficiently learn the craft. Many L.O.R.T. Theatres have a number of different Designers working for them during the course of a season. They will expose you to different styles and approaches to specific technical problems. You may even get to know one of these visiting artists well enough to have a first foot in the door towards working as their assistant when you are ready.

The other major difference between L.O.R.T. interns and apprentices in Summer Stock is probably pay. While it is true that L.O.R.T. Theatres are non-profit, most of them do understand that you must be able to live like a human being and that you have grown accustomed to eating. While you will not make a lot of money, if you are fortunate enough to be hired, you will probably be paid anywhere up to $150 per week. Often the theatres can be very helpful with housing. They may be able to place you in the extra room of one of their Board of Directors, or they may have worked out a deal with a local apartment building to keep a certain number of apartments filled all year round.

As mentioned above, these theatres operate on a much longer season. Some L.O.R.T. Theatres have programs for credit set up with local colleges and universities. The Repertory Theatre of St. Louis is on the campus of Webster University, and has a program of reciprocal benefit with the University. The Asolo State Theatre in Florida is able to have a program with Florida State

University, even though there is considerable distance between them. If the theatre does not have a specific program set up, it may be possible to arrange one. On the whole, however, the L.O.R.T. Theatres are in the market for people just out of school and beginning their lives in the theatre. They will assume that you have certain basic skills, are familiar with the long hours of hard work that the theatres demand and that you are dedicated to a quality product.

SHOWCASES AND WORKSHOPS

While theatre can and does occur in every area of the country, the three main centers are New York, Los Angeles and Chicago. These are the places which have the highest percentages of professional theatre talent. The people there desire to work and to have their work seen in hopes of earning a living. To that end, they have taken to developing showcases and workshops. Actors' Equity Association, the actors and Stage Managers' union, allows its members to work in these productions, as do the other theatrical unions. In Chicago they are known by the name "off-Loop," in Los Angeles they are referred to as "99-seat Waiver productions," referring to the waiver of full Equity contract in theatres with fewer than 100 seats. In Equity this waiver is described as the "Funded Theatre Code," but the theatres are referred to as "showcases" or "workshops." The idea behind all of these productions is the development of new talent, be they playwrights, actors, directors or designers. Everyone working on the project agrees to work for very little, if any, money. They hope that their work will be seen, appreciated and hired by a producer. Generally showcases involve some small stipend, to cover expenses, to the people working on them. Workshops are seldom, if ever, paid. Both of these forms fall under the heading of "off off-Broadway." While A.E.A. does not have jurisdiction over the theatres which use no union actors at all, it does control the majority of these productions, with stringent rules as to the amount of the expense stipend, hours, and the performer or Stage Manager's involvement in a subsequent commercial production of a given work. In New

York, there are about 80 theatres involved with these productions all year round. Some of these shows take place in beautiful and well equipped theatres. Some showcases are performed in big open rooms with folding chairs. Some are performed in store fronts. The productions may be classic, tried and true plays presented in new and exciting productions. The productions may be of totally new, realistic plays or they may be completely avant garde approaches to the theatrical experience. The one unifying need they all have is for dedicated and talented people to work on them. They are a very good place for the young theatre person to gain a variety of experience and to work with and learn from professionals. They quite often result in many people getting to know you and your work. As time goes by, you will find the theatrical community to be a very small place, and discover paying jobs as a result of showcase work. There are few Stage Managers, Designers and Technicians who have not worked in this arena at some point in their careers. More and more frequently, Broadway shows begin with showcase "tryouts," in New York, Chicago or Los Angeles. You are likely to return to this arena throughout your career as a Stage Manager or Designer.

SOURCES OF JOBS

No matter in which area of theatre you wish to work, you must be aware of where to find out about available jobs.

Probably the most obvious source for job opportunities goes unused. In most cities in the U.S. you have only to look in the local papers and the phone book. Community theatre, school and non-Equity productions are being done all over. A simple list of these places will serve as a wonderful place to begin. Very seldom does a theatre refuse help, and some theatres can afford to pay for it. Write or call these operations and ask to speak to the people in charge. Better yet, drop by and introduce yourself. These productions are frequently of high caliber, and you are looking for experience and a chance to grow in the theatre.

In New York, because of its importance to the industry, the sources are a little more focused. Every Thursday, two "trade papers," newspapers devoted entirely to the entertainment industry, are available on newstands. They can be subscribed to. *Back Stage* and *Show Business* each costs seventy-five cents. While the majority of the information in them is listings of auditions for actors, they can be a great help in finding out what is happening when and where. These pages list productions needing help, not only in New York City, but across the country. Each week, *Back Stage* has a special section which is concerned with design and technical positions. *Show Business* frequently has lists of theatres operating under various A.E.A. contracts, such as L.O.R.T. and Dinner Theatres. In late March or early April, *Back Stage* publishes an exhaustive list of the nation's Summer Theatres. Such listings are up-to-date sources for anyone working in the theatre. In addition to these papers, the weekly *Variety* lists shows in some process of production. The "what's happening where" guides in Manhattan newspapers will provide you with a list of showcase theatres. At the present time, the most complete listings are available in *The Village Voice,* and in *Other Stages,* a free publication distributed in off off-Broadway theatres.

In the midwest, Chicago is the main source of theatrical activity. Although most production information seems to spread by word of mouth, the arts sections of local suburban newspapers conscientiously lists auditions and production plans for area community theatres, and some off-Loop and L.O.R.T. companies.

While Los Angeles is still mainly a television and movie town, there has grown, of late, a considerable theatrical community. Many people have put their own money together to present 99-Seat Waiver Productions, the L.A. version of Showcases. There is a West Coast printing of *Back Stage.* Several other periodicals, including *Drama Logue, Casting Call, Daily Variety* and the *L.A. Weekly* all list openings for Designers and Technicians as a need arises.

T.C.G.

T.C.G., or the Theatre Communications Group, is an organization devoted to increasing communication between non-profit arts institutions. T.C.G. offers several services for the production-oriented theatre persons in search of work. Two of these services and an important T.C.G. publication should be known by the young Stage Manager, Technician or Designer.

The first service is *Artsearch*. This is a bi-weekly newsletter available by subscription. It advertises job openings and internships at arts institutions around the country, whether they are affiliated with T.C.G. or not. In a given issue, theatres, dance companies, community theatres, colleges and universities may advertise. Positions from Artistic Director to Carpenter to intern have been sought in *Artsearch*, Subscriptions cost $25, and can be obtained from T.C.G., 355 Lexington Ave., New York, NY 10017.

T.C.G. also maintains a referral service for Designers. Scenic and Costume Designers can file 35 mm slides of their work in a permanent slide library. T.C.G. also keeps a file of their resumes, and the resumes of Lighting Designers. The files are made available to prospective employers who are looking for Designers. The files are permanent; material can be removed from them only on the request of the Designer. T.C.G. also helps with career counseling for new graduates. They will assist you with the preparation of your file, and they will give suggestions as to where you must go to get started in the business.

Finally, T.C.G.'s *Theatre Profiles,* a directory of non-profit professional theatres, published bi-annually, is an excellent job resource. For nearly 170 theatres, seasons and artistic aims are described, photographs of productions are included, and there is some indication of the size of the staff and names of key personnel are given. T.C.G. is the best known and most diverse information service for the theatre professional. It is not the only one.

THEATRE ORGANIZATIONS

During your college years you are likely to come into contact with U/RTA, the University/Resident Theatre Association. U/RTA, now an independent organization, began as a branch of the American Theatre Association, the Theatre's professional association. Branches of A.T.A. concern themselves with Community Theatre, Children's

Theatre, Secondary School Theatre, Army Theatre, and University and College Theatre. U/RTA is most directly involved with entry level employment. As the name implies, U/RTA is allied with many educational institutions around the country. While it maintains no direct employment referral service, a duty assumed by A.T.A., U/RTA conducts annual auditions and interviews for Designers, Stage Managers and Technicians, among other theatre workers. The result can be graduate school acceptances, assistantships, or paid positions with its member organizations. These auditions are held each spring in New York, Chicago and Los Angeles. To take part in the auditions, you must be nominated by your college theatre department or by a professional theatre company. Once there, you must make a presentation to a group of potential employers. Any who are interested will call you back for a more personal interview.

REGIONAL THEATRE ORGANIZATIONS

The American Theatre Association has divided the country up into nine regions. Each of these has a regional theatre association. Some of these groups have been active for many years, and their annual conferences provide excellent job-seeking opportunities. The Southeastern Theatre Conference, or S.E.T.C., is such a regional organization, an alliance of theatres, outdoor dramas and academic institutions in the southeastern section of the country. They sponsor interview/auditions, similar to those of U/RTA, in September and March. They also keep in-house files of resumes for the use of prospective employers. This *Job Contact Service* is available by joining S.E.T.C. Dues are $20 per year, $10 for students, with a one time payment of $5 for joining the Job Contact Service. As a member, you will be given information about their conventions, during which job interviews will be scheduled. The Southwest Theatre Conference (S.W.T.C.) and New England Theatre Conference (N.E.C.) sponsor similar mass audition/interview sessions.

Similarly to the regional associations, most states in the union have a state theatre association, more or less active. Information about your state theatre association can be had from A.T.A., or from your school theatre department, which is likely to be a member. Some state theatre associations, like the regional organizations, schedule annual conferences at which time theatre employers within the state are available to meet with prospective employees.

The national organization, the American Theatre Association, has a Placement Service. Although many of their listings are for teachers of theatre, they also list non-teaching jobs at colleges and universities, internships, and occasionally jobs in industry. To affiliate with their Placement Service, you must first be a member of A.T.A. ($55 a year, $25 for retirees, $30 for students). For an additional payment of $20 per year you can receive their monthly Placement Bulletin, listing available positions. For $35 for the first year and $30 for each year thereafter, you are entitled to full membership in the Placement Service. A.T.A. will keep on file both your resume and up to nine letters of recommendation from previous employers. The $30 or $35 fee includes monthly copies of the Placement Bulletin.

The National Arts Jobbank publishes a newsletter 24 times a year, listing up to 100 jobs per issue. They list positions with many types of arts organizations, from theatres to symphonies, from salaried positions to internships. A subscription costs $24 for a year or $18 for a half year.

A recently established service of the U.S. Institute for Theatre Technology (U.S.I.T.T.) is the Theatre Design and Technology Clearinghouse. Listings are available of internships in the areas of Administration, Design, Technical Production, Costume Technology, Management (Stage Management and Production Assistance) and Manufacturing and Sales. Requests for copies of the listings must indicate which area or areas are desired, and be accompanied by a $3 handling fee for each area requested. You will receive an individualized computer printout containing detailed information about the opportunities offered by theatres or films which accept as interns bona fide students enrolled in an academic program of study, unlike L.O.R.T. internships, which are usually post-graduate positions. The Clearinghouse is much more an information service than a job placement service. However, since internships during the duration of a term or a summer are frequently a part of the requirements for a

B.F.A. or M.F.A. degree, it is a useful service, one that may help you secure experience and personal contact with people working in the business while you are still in school. In 1983, the Clearinghouse, although recently formed, represented over 120 theatres, organizations and firms. U.S.I.T.T., the sponsoring organization, is a professional society of theatre designers, technicians, administrators and consultants. It has a number of regional sections which plan activities throughout the year, and student sections at some universities. They publish a newsletter, a quarterly journal and sponsor an annual spring conference. Regular membership is $40 per year; $17.50 for students.

Many smaller, more localized organizations exist which can assist you in the search for work. Many have newsletters which mention job openings. The Alliance of Resident Theatres/New York (ART/NY) and the Los Angeles Theatre Alliance often print job openings available through their member theatres. Technical Assistance Project is an organization providing technical expertise to dance companies. They sometimes know of job openings for technicians. Nearly every organization which serves some facet of the theatrical community will be able to help you in your search for employment, if only on the basis of "here's-our-list-write-them."

Although you may be able to visit nearby theatres, to deliver a resume and request an interview, your first application to most places that you may work is usually by letter.

APPLYING FOR A JOB

At this point in your career, the point of seeking employment, you will have to become a salesperson. Like any salesperson, you will need a good product, an initial contact, a great deal of persistence and a lot of luck. You will need these qualities for the rest of your life. Let us assume that you have a good product—your skills and talent. Let us also assume that you have persistence, or you would not be trying to get a job in theatre in the first place. What do you need to make contact?

The Resume

The calling card for every member of the theatrical community is the resume. If there were one rule that people who want to work must follow, it would be: Never go anywhere near a job application without a resume! Sure, you can always tell someone who is interviewing you what you have done. But, after they have spoken with several hundred people, they may not remember you. If they have a piece of paper in front of them with your information on it, they have less excuse for not hiring you.

Keep your resume limited to one page. Most employers keep files on people in whom they are interested for the future, but they do not have unlimited file space. Often extra pages are simply thrown out. Make sure that your name, current address, telephone numbers and union affiliations, if any, are on the resume. Group all of your experience under precise headings. Broadway experience, when you have it, will go first, followed by regional, dinner, summer, showcase and school work. It is understandable that when you are beginning your career your only experience will be in school, community or amateur theatre. As time goes by and you update your resume, you will list that experience under Training or Academic. Your listing should be precise as possible without being wordy. List the name of the show, the producer or producing organization and the Director. List the precise job that you performed. Don't ever stretch the truth by calling yourself the Lighting Designer when you were the Electrician, or the Stage Manager when you ran props. That is not only dishonest, but also sure to be found out. The theatre is a very small world, and the person who is interviewing you is likely to know the people who were the Lighting Designer and the Stage Manager.

Near the bottom of your resume you should list any special skills or circumstances that might help you in the types of jobs for which you are applying. Such skills might include anything from an interest in painting to driving a car. If you have studied with an especially well known Designer, be sure to mention this.

All resumes should be typed on 8½″ x 11″ paper. A hand written resume simply shows your inexperience, and you run the risk of not having anyone able to read it. With each job it is acceptable to add that new notation in longhand, but print it, and never let more than a handful of jobs go by without updating your resume in typed format. You will be sending resumes to a great many places, so once you have copy that fits your needs, have a print shop run off a quantity of copies.

The Cover Letter

Do not just drop a resume in an envelope and send it off to each of the theatres on a list. Enclose a cover letter, typed, of course, telling the person in charge exactly the position or positions for which you wish to be considered. Mention that you have just finished school and are beginning your career, that you are in school and are interested in working during the summer, or mention your last job. Is there anything about the organization to which you are applying that particularly attracts you? (Schedule, part of the country, type of stage, kinds of plays done?) Say so, but do keep your cover letter concise and to the point. You should mention when you might be available for an interview, or to begin work. Mention that your resume is enclosed, and thank the person for his or her consideration. Whenever possible, address your cover letter to the proper person, by name. Letters beginning "Dear Mr. or Ms." are better than letters beginning "Dear Managing Director." Find *the* name to write to if you possibly can.

The Portfolio

Eventually, young Designers will receive an answer to one of their job inquiries, requesting that the Designer come for an interview. You will not be hired as a Designer on the basis of your resume alone. When you walk in the door for an interview, you will be expected to have a portfolio of your past work with you. URTA expects prospective Designers to present portfolios at their interviews. What can you show that will impress a prospective employer?

Even if your only experience is class projects, you will have sketches along the design process, renderings, elevations, color swatches and, if any of your work has been realized, photographs. Since young

Designers may be hired as assistants, a prospective Design-employer will need to know if you can draft. Good examples of different types of drafting are an important component of your portfolio. As you gain enough experience to be selective about what to include in your portfolio, do not feel compelled to include each and every piece of work that you have done. Work that you are proud of should be included. If it is possible within that parameter to include a range of classics and modern shows, plays and musicals, so much the better.

Photographs are an important part of the Designer's portfolio. It will likely mean becoming a somewhat competent photographer yourself, but it is important that you have photographs of each set or group of costumes that you design. They provide a record of your work, and, in a portfolio, in conjunction with renderings and sketches for the same piece of work, you communicate some idea of both what was conceived and agreed upon and what was actually built and completed.

A Costume Designer will bring photos and renderings of any projects in which they have been involved. Sketches might have swatches of fabric attached to them.

Some Designers, who have amassed a large body of work, keep the contents of their portfolio the same for all interviews, but also bring with them a slide projector and a small group of slides which show costumes or sets akin to the ones for which they are being inter-viewed.

Lighting and Sound Designers have a bit more difficulty showing their work, but they can show an understanding of the equipment they will use as well as a sense of organization in paper work from past projects. As with the Scenic Designer, examples of drafting should be included. A Sound Designer may wish to bring a tape recorder and a short sample tape.

BECOMING KNOWN

A famous Broadway Lighting Designer told us that "fully 90% of my work comes through friendly contacts." What he meant was that so often we hear of a possible job from friends in the business or people with whom we have worked. Often we make contact with a producer because he has heard of our work from friends. A job seeker in the theatre (and we are all job seekers for the majority of time) should track down any possible lead given to him or her from any source. The worst that a prospective employer can do is say *no*.

Finally, when you have secured a job, remember that it is easiest to find the second job while you are still working at the first. The theatre is a business of visibility; write to other producers while your present assignment gives you that visibility. Notify the people who may have said "Let me know when you're doing a show." You will be more confident when you are working, and a prospective employer may become more confident in your talents if he or she is able to see them demonstrated in production.

RELATED READING

Books. There are many books written about how to "do" theatre. Those that we have chosen to list here seem to us to augment this book by concentrating on the process of putting on plays, offering more detailed descriptions of available jobs.

Burris-Meyer, Harold and Edward C. Cole. *Scenery for the Theatre, The Organization, Processes, Materials and Techniques Used to Set the Stage.* 2nd Rev. Edition. Boston. Little, Brown and Company. 1972.

Burris-Meyer, Harold and Vincent Mallory./Revised edition. *Sound in the Theatre* New York. Theatre Arts Books. 1979.

Greenburg, Jan. *Theatre Careers:*A comprehensive guide to non-acting careers in the theatre. New York. Holt, Rinehart and Winston. 1983.

Gruver, Bert. *Stage Manager's Handbook.* Revised Edition. New York. Drama Book Publishers. 1972.

Ingham, Rosemary and Elizabeth Covey. *The Costumer's Handbook: How to Make All Kinds of Costumes.* Englewod Cliffs, NJ. Prentice-Hall, Inc. 1979.

Ingham, Rosemary and Elizabeth Covey. *The Costume Designer's Handbook.* Englewood Cliffs, NJ. Prentice-Hall, Inc. 1983.

Motley, *Theatre Props.* New York. Drama Book Publishers. 1976.

Rosenthal, Jean and Lael Wertenbaker. *The Magic of Light: The Craft and Career of Jean Rosenthal, Pioneer in Lighting for the Modern Stage.* New York and Boston. Theatre Arts Books and Little, Brown and Company. 1973.

Tompkins, Dorothy Lee. *Handbook for Theatrical Apprentices, A Practical Guide for All Phases of Theatre.* New York. Samuel Franch. 1962.

Periodicals—Newspapers

Back Stage (Weekly)
165 West 46th Street
New York, NY 10036

Show Business (weekly)
136 West 44th Street
New York, NY 10036

Variety (weekly)
154 West 46th Street
New York, NY 10036

Daily Variety
1400 N. Cahuenga Blvd.
Hollywood, CA 90028

The Hollywood Drama-Logue (weekly)
1456 North Gordon Street
Hollywood, CA 90028

Casting Call (weekly)
3365 Cahvenga Blvd. West
Los Angeles, CA 90068

Los Angeles Weekly
5325 Sunset Blvd.
Los Angeles, CA 90027

All of the above publications list theatre jobs available.

Periodicals—Magazines

Theatre Crafts (10 issues per year)
135 5th Ave.
New York, NY 10010

Theatre Design and Technology (quarterly)
330 West 42nd Street
New York, NY 10036

Lighting Dimensions (7 issues per year)
31706 South Coast Highway, Suite 302
South Laguna, CA 92677

ORGANIZATIONS

National Membership Organizations
American Theatre Association (ATA)
1010 Wisconsin Ave, NW
Washington, D.C. 20007

State and Regional Organizations;
Placement Service, Annual Conference.

U.S. Institute for Theatre Technology (USITT)
330 West 42nd Street
New York, NY 10036

Regional and Student Sections;
Internship Clearinghouse, Annual Conference.

Theatre, Film and Television Lighting Committee (TTFL)
Illuminating Engineering Society (IES)
345 East 47th Street
New York, NY 10017

University/Resident Theatre Association (U/RTA)
1540 Broadway—Suite 704
New York, NY 10036

Regional Organizations
New England Theatre Conference (NETC)
50 Exchange Street
Waltham, MA 02154

Southeastern Theatre Conference (SETC)
1209 W Market Street
Greensboro, NC 27412

Rocky Mountain Theatre Alliance (RMTA)
c/o Skyline Project
1331 18th St.
Denver, CO 80202

Service Organizations
The organizations listed below provide formal or informal assistance in job-finding.

Theatre Communications Group
355 Lexington Ave.
New York, NY 10017

Technical Assistance Project
American Dance Festival
1860 Broadway, Room 1112
New York, NY 10023

Alliance of Resident Theatres/New York
325 Spring Street
New York, NY 10013

Los Angeles Theatre Alliance
6253 Hollywood Blvd. Suite 312
Los Angeles, CA 90028

The National Arts Jobbank
141 East Palace Ave.
Santa Fe, NM 87501

SOURCES OF LISTS OF PRODUCING ORGANIZATIONS WHICH HIRE THEATRE DESIGNERS AND TECHNICIANS

We have included names, addresses and contact persons for Theme Parks, which are reasonably stable institutions. Since other theatres may come and go, or change managements, we have listed sources from which you may acquire up-to-date lists in these areas.

THEME PARKS

The Old Country/Busch Gardens
Entertainment Dept.
The Old Country, Busch Gardens
P.O. Drawer F-C
Williamsburg, Virginia 23185
The Dark Continent/Busch Gardens
Entertainment Dept.
The Dark Continent, Busch Gardens
3000 Busch Boulevard
Tampa, Florida 33612

Walt Disney World
Talent Booking Office
Walt Disney World Entertainment Division
P.O. Box 40
Lake Buena Vista, Florida 32830
Disneyland
Entertainment Division
Disneyland
1313 Harbor Blvd.
Anaheim, Calif. 92803
Opryland
Entertainment Dept.
Opryland, U.S.A.
2802 Opryland Drive
Nashville, Tennessee 37214
Hersheypark
Allan Albert
Hersheypark (Entertainment)
Hershey, Pennsylvania 17033
Magic Valley Village
John Henson, Entertainment Manager
Magic Valley Park
Bushkill, Pennsylvania 18324
Six Flags Great Adventure
Show Operations
Six Flags Great Adventure
P.O. Box 120
Jackson, N.J. 08527
Six Flags Over Texas
Show Operations
Six Flags Over Texas
P.O. Box 191
Arlington, Texas 76004-0191
Astroworld
Show Operations
Astroworld
9001 Kirby Drive
Houston, Texas 77054

Six Flags Over Georgia
Show Operations
Six Flags Over Georgia
P.O. Box 43187
Atlanta, Georgia 30378
Six Flags Over Mid-America
Show Operations
Six Flags Over Mid-America
Box 666
Eureka, Missouri 63025
Six Flags Magic Mountain
Show Operations
Six Flags Magic Mountain
P.O. Box 5500
Valencia, California 91355
Taft Attractions
Entertainment Department
1932 Highland Avenue
Cincinnati, Ohio 45219

REGIONAL THEATRES

Theatre Profiles, published biennially by Theatre Communications
Group (see Service Organizations above), lists performance schedules, artistic statements, names of Artistic and Managing Directors,
and other pertinent information for nearly 170 American Theatres.

SUMMER THEATRES

The Summer Theatre Guide from an Actor's Viewpoint, a pamphlet
compiled by John Allen and available from Summer Theatre Guide,
c/o On Board Answering Service, 35 West 45th Street, 6th Floor,
New York, NY 10036. Includes detailed information about 90 non-
Equity Summer Theatres, including contact persons and size of technical staff. *Back Stage* (see Newspapers listing above), in late March

or early April each year publishes an extensive listing of the names, addresses and producers of Equity and non-Equity Summer Theatres. Both *Back Stage* and *Show Business* publish listings of available Summer Theatre jobs.

OUTDOOR PAGEANTS

All Outdoor Pageants are members of the Institute for Outdoor Drama. Write the President of the Institute, Mark Sumner, at the Institute for Outdoor Drama, University of North Carolina, Chapel Hill, NC 27514 for a listing of Outdoor Dramas. (they are also included in the *Back Stage* listing). Institute members hold interviews and auditions at the Spring Convention of the Southeast Theatre Conference.

OFF OFF BROADWAY THEATRES

A list can be obtained from the Alliance of Resident Theatres/New York (see Service Organizations above)

DINNER THEATRES

Lists are occasionally published in *Back Stage* and *Show Business.*

VGM CAREER HORIZONS SERIES

CAREER PLANNING

Life Plan
Planning Your College
    Education

SURVIVAL GUIDES

High School Survival
    Guide
College Survival Guide

OPPORTUNITIES IN

*Available in both
paperback and hardbound
editions*
Accounting
Acting
Advertising
Airline Careers
Appraising Valuation
    Science
Architecture
Automotive Service
Banking
Beauty Culture
Biological Sciences
Book Publishing
Broadcasting
Building Construction
    Trades
Cable Television
Carpentry
Chemical Engineering
Chemistry
Chiropractic Health Care
Civil Engineering
Counseling & Guidance
Dance
Dental Care
Drafting

Data Processing
Electrical Trades
Electronic and Electrical
    Engineering
Energy Careers
Engineering Technology
Environmental Careers
Fashion
Film
Fire Protection Services
Food Services
Foreign Language
    Careers
Forestry
Free Lance Writing
Government Service
Graphic Communications
Health and Medical Careers
Hospital Administration
Hotel & Motel
    Management
Industrial Design
Interior Design
Journalism
Landscape Architecture
Law Careers
Law Enforcement
Library and Information
    Science
Machine Shop Trades
Magazine Publishing
Management
Marine & Maritime
Materials Science
Mechanical Engineering
Nursing
Occupational Therapy
Office Occupations
Opticianry
Optometry
Packaging Science

Paralegal Careers
Paramedical Careers
Personnel Management
Pharmacy
Photography
Physical Therapy
Podiatric Medicine
Psychiatry
Psychology
Public Relations
Real Estate
Recreation and Leisure
Refrigeration and
    Air Conditioning
Religious Service
Sales & Marketing
Secretarial Careers
Securities Industry
Sports & Athletics
Teaching
Technical
    Communications
Theatrical Design
    & Production
Transportation
Travel Careers
Veterinary Medicine
Writing Careers

WOMEN IN

*Available in both
paperback and
hardbound editions*
Communications
Engineering
Finance
Government
Management
Science
Their Own Business

VGM Career Horizons
A Division of National Textbook Company
4255 West Touhy Avenue
Lincolnwood, Illinois 60646-1975